THE LITTLE BOOK OF
HORSERACING

A HORSERACING A to Z

Written by Jonny Whetstone and Claire Welch

THE LITTLE BOOK OF
HORSERACING

This edition first published in the UK in 2006
By Green Umbrella

© Green Umbrella Publishing 2006

www.greenumbrella.co.uk

Publishers Jules Gammond, Tim Exell, Vanessa Gardner

Printed and bound in China

ISBN-13: 978-1-905009-59-6
ISBN-10: 1-905009-59-3

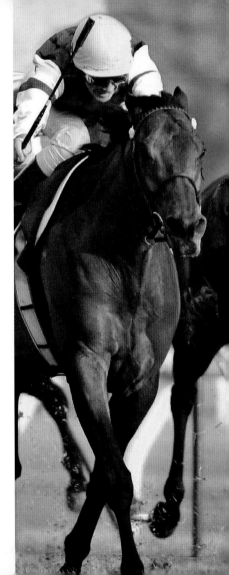

Contents

Aldaniti

BORN IN 1970, GELDING Aldaniti was named by his breeder Tommy Barron who used the first two letters from each of his grandchildren's first names (Alastair, David, Nicola and Timothy). Josh Gifford bought the gelding at Ascot sales and, after failing to sell him on, decided to race him in the novice hurdle at Ascot. The chestnut gelding beat the late Queen Mother's horse, Sunyboy, and his performance attracted Nick Embricos who purchased him the following day.

After failing to win any more races over hurdles, Aldaniti went lame at Sandown in January 1976 and it was to be 13 months before he was seen back on track when he finished third in the Hennessy Cognac Gold Cup. He was by now seven years old and had had victories at Ascot,

Leicester and Uttoxeter. Unfortunately, he was once again lame and had to tolerate seven months' rest.

He made a comeback in December 1978 and went on to claim third place in the 1979 Gold Cup, following it with a second in the Scottish Grand National. However, injuries once again blighted his potential and he spent most of 1980 recuperating.

Bob Champion had a great deal of faith in Aldaniti – they had been regular partners and Bob, facing his own battle with cancer, diagnosed in 1979, was determined that the young horse could win the Grand National. While Champion recovered in America, Aldaniti returned in February 1981 and won a valuable chase race, even though he was unconsidered at 14/1.

On 4 April that same year, Aldaniti faced 39 rivals at Aintree but he and Champion started at 10/1 second favourite. Aldaniti jumped into the lead at the 11th – but trainer and jockey thought it was too soon. The favourite, Spartan Missile was a formidable threat, but Aldaniti showed courage and won the Grand National by four lengths. He was retired immediately after the 1982 National where he fell at the first fence.

Aldaniti was honoured with a special 20th birthday party at Sandown Park Racecourse on 13 May 1999. It was a get-together for every legendary National Hunt horse still living, with the aim of raising £250,000 for the Bob Champion Cancer Trust.

Aldaniti made it into the news again in May 1996 when he ate a gold Polo mint from the palm of veteran horse-man Wilf Millam. Their particular party trick had been for the horse to take the polo gently from Wilf's lips – but he thought the sweet was a funny colour and just gave it to the horse. It turned out it was part of a promotion and was worth £1,000 – Wilf admitted that next time he would read the packet!

Aldaniti died in 1997 and is buried outside the stables where he spent his retirement.

ABOVE Aldaniti with Bob Champion in 1996

All Weather

ALL WEATHER

RIGHT The field in action on the all weather track at Southwell racecourse in Nottinghamshire – it doesn't have to be raining!

BELOW Racing on the new all-weather track at Kempton in 2006

ALL-WEATHER RACETRACKS first saw the light of day in Britain in 1989, and have since been regarded by some as a blessing, others – including many punters – as a nightmare. The plusses were soon obvious, as the sandy surface clearly withstood the rigours of the English weather far more readily than the conventional turf, allowing flat racing to take place all year round. Trainers were given the option, if required, of running horses throughout the winter and flat jockeys could find employment close to home.

From a betting point of view, it became more difficult to pick winners, because form from the turf is virtually useless when assessing a horse's chances on the all-weather; apart from anything else the conditions are more constant on the latter surface. With new Polytrack surfaces, turf and all weather are not dissimilar on form

The one thing that is certain is that the all-year option is not going to go away. In 2006, amidst much publicity, Kempton Park unveiled its new all-weather track, adding it to Wolverhampton, Southwell and Lingfield as courses with similar facilities.

Archer

FRED ARCHER, THE SON OF GRAND National-winning jockey William Archer, was born at Cheltenham in 1857. Apprenticed to Mathew Dawson at Newmarket at the age of 11 years, he rode his first winner when just 13.

Dawson soon recognised Archer's potential and made him his stable jockey in 1873. He became Champion Jockey in the following year and remained so for the 13 years until his death. Also in 1874 he won his first Classic, the 2,000 Guineas, on Atlantic for Lord Falmouth, who afterwards retained Archer as his jockey.

The combination of Falmouth, Dawson and Archer carried all before them in the major races and soon Archer, a quiet man with a ruthless will to win, became the public's hero. Nicknamed the 'Tin Man', he won a remarkable 2,748 races, including 21 Classics. One of his five Derby victories saw him ride the winner, Bend Or, with one arm in a splint after being severely savaged by a horse on the gallops.

In 1884 he married Matt Dawson's niece and moved into Falmouth House the home he had built in Newmarket. However, his personal life reached rock bottom when his first child died, followed by his wife while giving birth to a second.

Archer threw himself into riding but, continually battling with his weight, he became ill with typhoid fever. Although recovering from his illness, he shot himself in a fit of depression in 1886, aged just 29 years.

ABOVE Fred Archer looking dapper in a suit, in 1885

Arkle

BORN 19 APRIL 1957, ARKLE dominated steeplechasing in the early part of the 1960s. Bought for 1,150 guineas by Anne, Duchess of Westminster, the bay gelding named after a Scottish mountain was given plenty of time to develop. His sire Archive was a failure as a racehorse but his dam Bright Cherry had been a good steeplechase winner.

He first ran in December 1961 and finished unplaced on both starts in bumpers. But when switched to hurdles he won two races. Arkle was improving all the time and, when he ran over fences in the 1962-63 season, he proved to be the best novice chaser in England and Ireland by winning at Cheltenham and Fairyhouse.

Trained in Ireland by the great Tom Dreaper and ridden by Pat Taafe, Arkle

came to England to take on 1962 Gold Cup winner Mill House in the following year's Hennessy Gold Cup. Though receiving weight from his opponent, Arkle was beaten. However, he gained his revenge at Cheltenham in the Gold Cup of 1964, beating Mill House by five lengths before winning the Irish National under top weight and then handing another beating to Mill House in the Hennessy, carrying 12 stone seven pounds.

Arkle went on to make it three Cheltenham Gold Cups in a row, adding another Hennessy Gold Cup, a King George VI Chase by a distance and a Whitbread Gold Cup carrying 12 stone seven pounds and giving 35 pounds to his nearest rival. He had carried 12 stone seven pounds in all his last handicaps and only Stalbridge Colonist, receiving 35 pounds, beat him in the Hennessy of 1966.

In what turned out to be his last race, Arkle was beaten by a length by Dormant in the 1966 King George VI Chase. He had fractured the pedal bone

of his hoof but still managed to finish the race. He retired in 1968, the winner of 27 of his 35 races. Timeform named him the 'Greatest Steeplechaser ever'.

Ascot

QUEEN ANNE FIRST USED ASCOT Heath in Berkshire for riding in the early part of the eighteenth century. She ordered the building of the racecourse, then known as East Cote, and the first meeting took place on Saturday 11 August 1711. The first event staged was Her Majesty's Plate, contested by any horse over the age of six years old and running over a distance of four miles.

BELOW Two women dressed in typical Ascot fashion in 1933

Regular meetings were held at Ascot until Queen Anne's death in 1714. But apart from George II's son, the Duke of Northumberland, there was no great interest shown in Ascot from the Royal Family until the reign of George III. He was responsible for making the meeting fashionable and introduced the Royal Enclosure in the 1790s. Situated about 30 miles from central London in the Berkshire countryside, the racecourse now bears little resemblance to those early days.

The highlight of the course calendar is the five-day Royal Ascot Meeting, held in the third week of June, when crowds of over 50,000 are present on most days. A host of group races and top handicaps are hotly contested during this week including the Queen Anne Stakes, St James' Palace Stakes, Coventry Stakes, Coronation Stakes, Queen Mary and Hardwicke Stakes.

The Ascot Gold Cup on the Thursday is the centrepiece of the event and tickets for this day inevitably sell out in advance. This is also called Ladies' Day and is the high point in the fashion stakes. For each day of the Royal Meeting, the Queen and her guests make a procession down the course in open

ABOVE The new Ascot grandstand nearing completion in 2005, with horses training in the foreground

horse-drawn carriages to the Royal Box before the opening race. George IV first introduced the custom in 1825.

The Queen, a great supporter of racing, has enjoyed success at Royal Ascot week, having amassed a total of 19 winners. Tradition has it that when a royal winner passes the winning post, the male race-goers toss their top hats in the air and shout 'hats off to the Queen'.

Other prestigious races are held during the year. In July the King George VI and Queen Elizabeth Diamond Stakes, run over 1½ miles, sees the first important all-age contest at that distance. In September races such as the Diadem Stakes, Hoover Fillies Mile, Royal Lodge Stakes and Queen Elizabeth II Stakes make another top-class meeting. National Hunt racing of a high standard also takes place during the winter months. But, for many, nothing can top the excitement, glamour and sport of Royal Ascot week.

Best Mate

THREE-TIME CHELTENHAM GOLD Cup winner Best Mate was always regarded as out of the ordinary – even his cautious trainer Henrietta Knight admitted 'He's a bit special' after his first novice hurdle at Cheltenham in November 1999.

Further success followed at Sandown before he came up against the brilliant but injury-prone Monsignor. Best Mate gave him a good race at Sandown, losing by only two and a half lengths. In 2000, Best Mate tasted victory at Aintree where he comfortably beat Martin Pipe's hurdler Copeland.

On 17 October 2000 the five year-old made his debut over fences at Exeter. The first three horses to finish that day were Best Mate, Bindaree and Shooting Light, and within the next 18 months they also went on to win the Thomas Pink Gold Cup, the Grand National and the Cheltenham Gold Cup. A further victory followed at Cheltenham, where his main rival Dusk Duel slipped. Knight had been gaining attention in the press with references to Best Mate possibly measuring up to the legendary Arkle.

He had a further victory at Sandown on 1 February 2001, but his claims as champion novice chaser were never fulfilled as restrictions over foot and mouth ensured that the Cheltenham Festival in 2001 was cancelled.

Best Mate won the Haldon Gold Cup at Exeter the following season and, as he

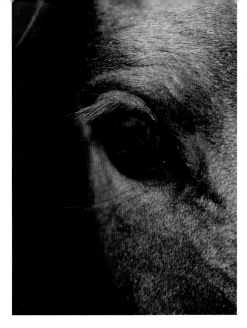

ABOVE A beautiful close-up of Best Mate's right eye

was unbeaten over fences, was now 10/1 for the Gold Cup. The 2001 King George VI Chase at Kempton had eight horses all capable of winning, but the race was to prove once and for all that Best Mate was worthy of that elusive Gold Cup. Ridden by AP McCoy, he finished a close second behind Florida Pearl.

There were 18 horses lined up for the 2002 Cheltenham Gold Cup and Best Mate had odds of 7/1. Best Mate with jockey Jim Culloty picked up the leaders as they turned for home and, as Istabraq bowed out, crossed the line to win.

No horse had won two Gold Cups since L'Escargot, more than 30 years before, and Best Mate faced rivalry from Irish novice Beef Or Salmon. His rival fell early on and he smoothly took the lead, winning by an easy ten lengths to register his second Gold Cup.

The following year saw him complete the treble and end any dispute that Best Mate was the best horse since Arkle. Sadly, Best Mate collapsed and died during a race at Exeter in November 2005.

Betting

WITH HORSERACING BECOMING ever more popular and the dreaded betting tax a distant memory, bookmakers both on and off course can look forward to a reasonably rosy future. In the twenty-first century we can virtually place a wager on any sporting event we wish, but for many punters 'having a bet' means one sport only – horseracing.

To a non-participant, the betting process might look daunting, given that the combinations of bets available can involve more than one horse at a number of different meetings. There are win, doubles and trebles, place doubles and trebles, yankees and all kinds of bets that can bamboozle the confused punter coming to the sport for the first time.

In fact the terminology counts for little nowadays, as betting shops are now quite welcoming establishments with trained staff only too pleased to sort out any problems their customers may have. Anxious to take your money over the counter, they will explain exactly how to make out a betting slip to accommodate your particular requirements. Betting shops are to found in

RIGHT Taking bets at Newmarket in 1936

BELOW A queue outside a new betting shop in south London, after they had been made legal in 1961

most local high streets and offer as close an experience to live racing as is possible off course, with television screens covering multiple race meetings on any one day. The busiest days of the year are always when the Derby and Grand National are run.

On course, placing a bet can be made at closer quarters via the many bookmakers to be found under their brightly covered umbrellas or on the Tote. There is now the added

attraction of the internet, with operations like Betfair offering online exchange betting.

The Tote was originally set up as an alternative to starting-price betting with bookmakers, its profits being ploughed back into the sport. Tote betting was unveiled in 1929 and has rarely looked back since.

Until 1972, the Tote had certain restrictions placed upon its activities but thereafter operated under the same conditions as any other bookmaker and consequently Tote betting shops became a feature countrywide.

Tote betting terminals can be found in over 4000 bookmakers and in 2002 the TotebetXpress internet betting service was launched, yet another service for their thousands of registered clients who were already placing bets by phone. The Levy Board which oversees the Tote has its members appointed by the government.

Breeders' Cup

HELD IN THE AUTUMN OF EACH year, the Breeders' Cup Championships first took place in 1984. Founded by John R Gaines in 1982 to create true championship races that would attract the best horses from all over the world; it has more than succeeded in this aim.

BELOW The pack makes the turn during the 2005 Breeders' Cup in October 2005 at Belmont Park in Elmont, New York

Races are run on the turf and dirt with a prize of at least $1 million and competition is extremely tough. The Breeders' Cup carries a top prize of $4 million and is held at a different race-track every year at such venues as Churchill Downs, Santa Anita, Belmont Park, Gulfstream Park and Hollywood Park. It was held for the first time outside the United States in 1996 when it was hosted by the Woodbine Racetrack, Toronto.

Memorable past winners have been Cigar and Arazi, while the likeable Tiznow holds the record for most prize money won, at $4,960,000, part of which was won in 2000 when holding off Aidan O'Brien's tough Irish challenger Giant's Causeway. However England and Ireland have made many successful raids on Breeders' Cup prizes with the super filly Pebbles in 1985, Pilsudski, Singspiel, High Chaparral, Royal Academy and latterly the ultra-consistent Ouija Board.

Brigadier Gerard

BRIGADIER GERARD WAS FOALED in 1968. Owned and bred by John and Jean Hislop, he soon became one of the most popular racehorses of the Twentieth Century. Trained by Dick Hern at West Ilsley, he first ran as a two year-old in June 1970 and was unbeaten in that season, the climax of which was the Middle Park Stakes at Newmarket. As a three-year-old he won the 2,000 Guineas on his debut, beating My Swallow and Mill Reef, who went on to win the Derby that year. Ridden beautifully by the stylist Joe Mercer, he extended his unbeaten run to 10, winning the top mile events before finishing the season with victory in the 1¼ mile Champion Stakes.

The following season, aged four, he won another five races of the highest quality, including the Eclipse and then, running over a distance of 1½ miles for the first time, the prestigious King George VI & Queen Elizabeth Diamond Stakes. In August at York he suffered his only defeat in the Benson and Hedges Gold Cup at the hands of the 1972 Derby winner Roberto, trained by Vincent O'Brien. There then followed two more victories in the Queen Elizabeth II Stakes and the Champion Stakes at Newmarket.

A most popular horse said by his trainer, Dick Hern to be 'very sound and never sick', Brigadier Gerard retired to stud duties but was, sadly, not a successful sire. He died in 1989.

BELOW Joe Mercer riding Brigadier Gerard to victory in the 1972 Queen Elizabeth II stakes at Ascot. (The horse behind is Sparkler, ridden by Lester Piggott)

Carson

BELOW Carson riding Tajannub at Royal Ascot in 1994

WILLIE CARSON WAS BORN IN Stirling, Scotland, on 16 November 1942. Despite a slow start to his career, Carson's determination paid off, and with his energetic racing style and will to win he developed into one of the finest jockeys in racing history.

He is one of a select handful of top jockeys to win the Derby on more than three occasions and, for all his achievements, winning the Derby is one of his most prized moments. Willie Carson has five championships, 17 English Classics (including wins on Troy 1979, Nashwan 1989 and Salsabil 1990), and has a career total of 3,828 winners. He is also the fourth highest winning jockey in British racing history after Piggott, Richards and Eddery.

As success did not come easily to Carson, he has readily admitted in the past that there were times when he nearly quit the sport. However, his drive gave him four Derby victories, the first of which was riding Troy, considered one of the top three horses he ever rode, in 1979.

Since his retirement from racing in 1997, Carson has remained actively

involved within the racing industry and was European racing manager for the Thoroughbred Corporation as well as a horseracing pundit for the BBC. He also owns and runs Minster Stud, which was established in 1980 on the site of the former Ampney Stud (with 55 acres) situated in the Cotswolds. Carson later acquired a further 100 acres and the stud has its own borehole.

Carson first began buying mares as early as the 1960s on the advice of Bernard van Cutsem. The highlight of the stud was Minster Son, ridden by Carson, who won the 1988 St Leger – which made Willie the only jockey to breed and ride a Classic winner.

The other passion in his life is football and he played against Leeds and Scotland's Billy Bremner when they were both kids in Sterling. He was too small to become a professional, but even while developing his interest in riding he was watching football. He managed to fulfil his dream, at least in part, when he became chairman of Swindon Town FC in 2001.

ABOVE Carson, in the centre in white shirt and dark spots, at the 1980 Epsom Derby, which he won on Nesbit

Cecil

HENRY CECIL WAS BORN in 1943, along with twin brother David, and was the stepson of royal trainer Sir Cecil Boyd-Rochfort. In 1964 he became his assistant at Freemason Lodge, Newmarket, where such horses as Meld, Aureole, Pall Mall, Above Suspicion and Alcide had been trained.

On his stepfather's retirement, Cecil took up the reins, and in 1968, his first season, won the Eclipse with Wolver Hollow. With an Irish 1,000 Guineas victory under his belt courtesy of Cloonagh in 1973, Cecil trained his first English Classic winner when Bolkonski, ridden by Frankie Dettori's father, Gianfranco, won the 2,000 Guineas of 1975 at odds of 33/1.

That was to be the first of a collection of 23 Classic victories, including four Derbys with Slip Anchor (1985) Reference Point (1987), Commander in Chief (1993) and Oath (1999).

Renowned for his skill in training fillies, Cecil has won the Oaks seven times and won the Fillies Triple Crown with Sheikh Mohammed's Oh So Sharp in 1985. Royal Ascot has always been a happy hunting ground and four Ascot Gold Cups were won between 1979 and 1982, Le Moss and Ardross sharing the victories between them.

From his Warren Place Stable in Newmarket, where he moved in 1976 on the retirement of father-in-law Sir Noel Murless, Henry Cecil has been Champion Trainer ten times. Although his association with Sheikh Mohammed ended in 1995, and the deaths of owners such as Jim Joel and Lord Howard de Walden have reduced his firepower, Cecil remains one of Britain's most popular trainers.

RIGHT Henry Cecil at Newmarket in 1988

BELOW Cecil poses with the Award of Merit at the Cartier Racing Awards in 2005

Champion

IN 1948, BOB CHAMPION WAS BORN into a hunting family. His father was huntsman to the Cleveland, Yorkshire, so Bob began riding at an early age. He rode his first point-to-point winner at the age of 15 before joining National Hunt racing with Toby Balding at Weyhill. He has since ridden for many top trainers including Josh Gifford, and gained much experience riding in America.

He was shocked to learn in 1979 that he had testicular cancer and, according to the two doctors who broke the news to him, only eight months to live unless he underwent an immediate intensive course of chemotherapy. Bob spent much of 1980 recuperating from cancer in the US, but his interest in Aldaniti, who had suffered extensive injuries and time away from the racecourse, never waned.

By April 1981, both Bob and Aldaniti, trained by Josh Gifford, had recovered and partnered for the Grand National on 4th April. Aldaniti took the lead by the 11th fence, and was the first winner since Sundew in 1957 to lead throughout the final circuit.

Bob retired from racing in 1983 after winning some 500 races – major wins include the Tote Ider Chase, the Hennessy Cognac Gold Cup, the Black & White Hurdle, the SGB Hurdle and the Whitbread Trial Chase. He received his MBE in 1983 and formed the Bob Champion Cancer Trust which has raised millions of pounds for cancer research. His life was portrayed in *Champion's Story*, a book that was later made into a film starring John Hurt. Bob is an accomplished after-dinner speaker.

ABOVE Champion reunited wiith Aldaniti in 1995

Channon

LIKE MANY PROFESSIONAL footballers, Mick Channon has always enjoyed the thrills and spills of horseracing. The difference with Channon is that he has made a second career as a trainer following his retirement from playing.

RIGHT Channon the trainer at Doncaster in 1997

BELOW Mick Channon in his football-playing days

Born on 28 November 1948 in Orcheston, Wiltshire, Michael Roger Channon made his first-team debut for Southampton at the age of 17 and broke through into the England team in 1972, finishing his international involvement in 1977 with 21 goals from 46 appearances. The high point of his career was helping Southampton to the 1976 FA Cup and he later played for Manchester City, Newcastle United, Bristol Rovers, Norwich City (winning the 1985 League Cup) and Portsmouth.

His horseracing career really took off when, after a spell as an assistant trainer, he became a licensed trainer in 1990 with ten horses. A move to the Queen's former stables in Newbury in 1999 enabled him to increase his tally to around 200 and he now trains at West Ilsley.

His first Group One success was with Piccolo in the 1994 Nunthorpe Stakes and in 2002 he topped the 100-winner mark for the first time, ending the season with more than £1.5m in prize money.

Channon, now one of the sport's most respected trainers, has yet to win one of the Classics but retains contacts from his footballing days and has trained horses for the likes of Kevin Keegan, Alan Ball and Sir Alex Ferguson.

Cheltenham

THE FIRST STEEPLECHASE AT Cheltenham was held in 1841 where the winner was Lottery, winner of the 1839 Grand National. The present course, where the Cheltenham Gold Cup is run, was laid out in 1902 and became the permanent venue for the four-mile National Hunt Steeplechase in 1911.

The Cheltenham Gold Cup was instituted in 1924, offering the chance for long-distance chasers to compete against each other under level terms in a weight-for-age race. Red Splash won the Gold Cup with prize money of £685. At first it was considered a training race on the way to the Grand National, but it became a prestigious race in its own right and is now recognised as the championship of steeplechasing.

Racing at Cheltenham did not always enjoy such prestige. During the 1820s, there were several years of protests and demonstrations from the parish priest, the Rev Francis Close, who warned his congregations against the evils of gambling. In 1829 rocks and empty bottles

were thrown at the horses and riders and 12 months later, the grandstand was burned down. Racing in Cheltenham resumed around 1841.

The first course at Prestbury Park was mapped out in 1865. It was bought by Baring Bingham in 1898 who re-established racing in the town. His idea was to rebuild a grandstand and erect rails around the course. Four years later in 1902, a huge two-day festival was held to mark the re-opening of Prestbury Park and, within a further two years, the course was established as

ABOVE The winning enclosure during the Cheltenham Festival in 1990

a major racing venue. Two years' later, Cheltenham again had a first with its inaugural Champion Hurdle which was run over two miles.

In 1934, Golden Miller, known affectionately as 'The Miller', became the only horse ever to win the Aintree Grand National and the Cheltenham Gold Cup in the same season. This amazing horse was to win a record total of five Gold Cups over a four-year

period. Three other horses, Cottage Rake (1948-50), Arkle (1964-66) and Best Mate (2002-04) have won the race three times consecutively. Best Mate has since been immortalised in a life-size bronze statue.

By 1949, the Festival meeting, which had been extended to three days, had become the highlight of the National Hunt season. The Festival, held in March, continued uninterrupted until 2001 when, for the first time in 50 years, it was cancelled due to foot and mouth restrictions. In 2005, the Festival was extended to four days and more than 270,000 race-goers now attend annually.

The 2005-06 season was another memorable period for jump racing, with AP McCoy retaining his title as Champion Jockey and War of Attrition winning the Cheltenham Gold Cup. Runners in the Cup must be five years old or above to run the three miles and 2.5 furlongs. Sadly nine horses died during the 2006 Festival and the Jockey Club and RSPCA, along with Cheltenham Racecourse officials, are looking at ways in which to reduce the risks to horses at this otherwise world-class venue.

Classics

THERE ARE FIVE CLASSIC RACES run in a season. These events, for three year-olds only, were first run in the late 1700s and early 1800s.

The St Leger was founded in 1776 and run at Doncaster on Cantley Common. Two years later the race moved to its present home at Turf Moor, Doncaster, and took on the name of local sportsman Lt General Anthony St Leger. Run over a distance of one mile six furlongs and 127 yards, the race is open to both colts and fillies, carrying nine stone and eight stone nine pounds respectively. This race, run as the final Classic each year, makes up the final leg of the Triple Crown.

In 1779 the Oaks, a mile and a half race for fillies only, was run for the first time at Epsom and was won by the Earl of Derby's Bridget. The Earl had founded the race which took the name of his Epsom house. All the fillies carry a weight of nine stone and, although they can compete against colts in 2,000 Guineas, Derby and St Leger, their male counterparts cannot take them on in the 1,000 Guineas or the Oaks.

Some fillies have been strong enough to take on the colts and beat them, namely Eleanor (1801), Blink Bonny (1857), Signorinetta (1908) and Fifinella (1916).

With the Oaks being the second leg of the Fillies' Triple Crown, just over a double handful of horses have achieved it, such as Pretty Polly, Sun Chariot, Meld and Oh So Sharp, in 1985, being the

BELOW Kieron Fallon and Virginia Waters leave the field behind them to land The Ultimatepoker.com 1,000 Guineas Stakes Race run at Newmarket in 2005

ABOVE Kieron Fallon on Golan lands the Sagitta 2000 Guineas Stakes at Newmarket in 2001

RIGHT Richard Quinn rides Princess Cleo to victory in the Class 2 DBS St Leger Yearling Stakes at Doncaster Races in 2005

most recent. However, Sceptre won four Classics outright in 1902 and Formosa in 1868 won the Fillies' Triple Crown, but also dead-heated with Moslem for the 2,000 Guineas.

The Derby, named after the twelfth Earl of Derby, was first run in 1780 and is open to colts and fillies carrying nine stone and eight stone nine pounds respectively. As the Oaks is run over a distance of 1½ miles, Benjamin Disraeli named the race the Blue Riband of the Turf and many great horses have won it

The 2,000 Guineas, run over one mile at Newmarket, takes place in early May. Colts carry 9 stone while fillies, which rarely run in it, carry eight stone nine pounds. A prize of 2,000 Guineas was won by Wizard in 1809, and thereafter the name of the race remained.

The very best have won this race on the way to Derby glory and use the 2,000 Guineas distance of one mile as a stepping-stone to the 1½ of the Epsom Classic. Ormonde, Isinglass, Pommern, Royal Palace and Nijinsky are just a few to do this.

The 1,000 Guineas, also run at Newmarket over one mile for three year-old fillies only, was first won by Christopher Wilson's Charlotte in 1814. Held like the 2,000 Guineas on the Rowley Mile, the roll call of fine fillies to take the race includes Sceptre, Pretty Polly, Sun Chariot, Meld, Pebbles, Petite Etoile and Oh So Sharp.

Colours

SHOULD YOU BE FORTUNATE enough to become a racehorse owner, you must not only register your name but a set of colours must be allocated to you before your horse can run.

The family firm of Weatherbys collects all data concerning racing and is responsible for all registration; compiling information from entries of races to weights, draw, jockeys etc on behalf of the British Horseracing Board.

In 1762, a list of 19 colours were issued by the Jockey Club that helped the owner to recognise their own horses in running. At that time all riders wore a plain black cap, but today a variety of colours are used with differing patterns of stripes, hoops, stars, checks, spots, diamonds and quarters. The jackets and sleeves carry an even greater choice of pattern with crossbelts, halves, chevrons, seams, epaulets, braces, and many more, to make up 27 forms available.

There are 18 colours to choose from, plus another seven that are 'cherished' and available only through auction. Plain colours are much sought after as they have all been taken up, but when they are sold make upwards of £50,000.

The straw colours of the Duke of Devonshire are one of the original colours remaining from the first issue in 1762. Godolphin carry all-blue colours, while their mighty rivals Coolmore across the Irish Sea carry the all-dark blue colours of Sue Magnier. All in all, racing is a colourful world.

ABOVE Colours can be very distinctive. This is Italian Frankie Dettori

Derby

Derby

RIGHT Epsom grandstand in 1836, with Derby winner Bay Middleton being led past

BELOW Race-goers dressed for the occasion at the 1990 Derby

NAMED AFTER THE 12TH EARL OF Derby, who tossed a coin with Sir Charles Bunbury to determine this honour, this Classic was first run in 1780 on Epsom Downs.

Although losing out on the name of the race, Bunbury had the pleasure of owning the first winner, Diomed. Lord Derby had to wait until 1787 before he won it with Sir Peter Teazle.

Run over a mile and half in the first week of June, it remains the most sought-after prize in a three year-old's Classic year. Open to colts and fillies and run on Epsom's switchback track, it provides a thorough test of a horse's ability and temperament with its vast crowds and funfairs surrounding the course.

The race has had its share of drama. In 1844 the first horse past the post, Running Rein, was found on closer inspection to be Maccabeus who was, in fact, a four year-old. He was disqualified and the race awarded to Orlando.

In 1913 Emily Davison, leader of the suffragette movement, dashed out on the course at Tattenham Corner and brought down Anmer, owned by King George V. Miss Davison died two days later in hospital, but jockey Herbert Jones was unhurt. The race was won by 100/1 outsider Aboyeur after first past the post Craganour was disqualified for bumping and boring.

Larkspur's victory in 1962 was gained after eight of the runners came down in a horrific pile-up when Romulus struck the heels of another horse. The Derby left its home during the first and second World Wars when it was run on the July course at Newmarket.

The most successful jockey in the race, winning it nine times, was Lester Piggott, a master of the Epsom course and the housewives' choice when it came to having a bet. It took Gordon Richards, the winner of 26 championships, 27 attempts before Pinza won the coveted prize for him in 1953.

Many great horses have won the Derby over the years. Sea Bird's effortless victory on the bridle in 1965 was memorable, as was Nijinsky in 1970 and Mill Reef in 1971. Shergar destroyed the opposition in 1981, winning by a record ten lengths under 19 year-old jockey Walter Swinburn.

More recent winners Sinndar (2000), High Chaparral (2002) and Motivator (2005) have helped maintain the race's great worldwide reputation. Although there are many top international prizes to be won, the Epsom Derby remains the race that breeders, owners, trainers and jockeys most want to win.

Desert Orchid

DESERT ORCHID WAS FOALED IN 1979. Bred by Jimmy Burridge from his hunter mare Flower Child and sired by Grey Mirage, there were no great expectations as to his racing career.

A grey gelding who as the years passed turned whiter, the horse was sent to be trained at Whitsbury, Hampshire by David Elsworth, a multi-talented trainer who had enjoyed success ranging from group winners on the flat to National winners over jumps.

Desert Orchid's career began to take off in his second season when, partnered by regular jockey Colin Brown, he won six of his eight starts over hurdles. Only once was he unplaced.

The horse, an adoring public knew as 'Dessie', was headstrong and slightly quirky but had been brilliantly handled by Elsworth, head lad Rodney Boult and stable lass Janice Coyle. Their patience began to pay off as he started his chasing career, winning his first four races in 1985.

In 1986, ridden now by Simon Sherwood, Dessie won his first King George VI Chase at Kempton. Thought

RIGHT Lester Piggott parades on Desert Orchid before racing at Wincanton

BELOW A portrait of Desert Orchid, taken in 1988

by many to be better at two miles, he dispelled those ideas with this victory. He went on to win the King George VI Chase a further three times in 1988, 1989 and 1990.

1988 saw him finish second to Pearlyman in the two-mile Queen Mother Champion Chase at Cheltenham, but he then showed his versatility by winning over three miles at Aintree before making all the running in the Whitbread Gold Cup at Sandown over three miles and five furlongs.

Desert Orchid's style of racing, a com-

bination of bold front running and fearless jumping, battered the opposition into submission. But if the opposition got close enough to him to take him on, he would fight to the end. After winning the Tingle Creek at Sandown and the King George VI Chase at Kempton, he showed that courage in the 1989 Cheltenham Gold Cup. In ground described as heavy and over three and a quarter miles, Dessie slogged it out to beat Yahoo by 1½ lengths. Given a great ride from his now-regular pilot Simon Sherwood, he had achieved a marvellous victory in conditions not ideal for him and at a course he'd never won on before.

Sherwood retired that season, having enjoyed nine unforgettable triumphs on his old friend. He was succeeded by Richard Dunwoody, who described Desert Orchid as the 'best horse he had sat on'. The story continued with two more victories in the King George VI (1989 and 1990) and an Irish National.

Now in happy retirement, he stands alongside Arkle and Red Rum as the most popular steeplechaser to grace the turf.

ABOVE Desert Orchid (centre) jumping a fence on his way to winning the Cheltenham Gold Cup race in 1989

Dettori

THE SON OF CLASSIC-winning jockey Gianfranco Dettori, Lanfranco, or Frankie as he is better known, was born in Italy in December 1970. Working in racing stables from the age of 13 in Italy, he came to England to serve his apprenticeship with Luca Cumani in Newmarket. He rode his first winner on Lizzy Hare at Goodwood in 1987.

After becoming Champion Apprentice in 1989, he was appointed first jockey to Luca Cumani, who had won the 1988 Derby with Khayasi, taking over from Ray Cochrane. This move gave Dettori the chance of riding top horses in top races and started to put him on the map. He then joined John Gosden, who trained for Sheik Mohammed, in Newmarket. Frankie became Champion Jockey in 1994, and with the mighty Godolphin Organisation behind him won the Championship again in 1995.

Classic success came his way with Balanchine, Moonshell, Classic Cliché, Mark of Esteem, Shantou and, with the likes of Halling taking Group One races, and Barathea a Breeders' Cup, Dettori was flying. After winning the King George VI & Queen Elizabeth Diamond Stakes, Lammtarra also provided him with his first Prix de L'Arc de Triomphe in 1995.

But with all these big-race successes, it was on a Saturday afternoon in September at Ascot's seven-race meeting in 1996 that made him world-renowned. The meeting was no run-of-the-mill event, but the highly competitive Ascot September meeting with top-class horses.

Dettori won the opener, the Cumberland Lodge Stakes on Godolphin's Wall Street, the Diadem Stakes by a short head on Diffident and then took the Queen Elizabeth II Stakes

RIGHT Frankie Dettori and Bahamian Ballet racing at Windsor in 2005

BELOW Dettori and his wife, Catherine, at Newbury in 2004

on Mark of Esteem – three from three for Godolphin as well. Decorated Hero won the Tote Festival Handicap for his old boss John Gosden before Fatefully gave Godolphin their fourth winner and Dettori his fifth.

By this time there was a real buzz and, by the time Lochangel, trained by Ian Balding had won the sixth in the Blue Seal Stakes, the impossible dream of riding seven winners on a card was very much a reality. The final race had a big field for the two-mile handicap; Dettori was riding top weight Fujiyana Crest for Michael Stoute.

On the morning of the race, a 12/1 price had been a true reflection of his chances. But now, with the bookmakers in serious trouble with liabilities of thousands and thousands for accumulators, the horse went of at a starting price of 2/1 favourite.

As Dettori led the field on the first circuit past the stands the crowd was getting louder and louder. Incredibly Fujiyana Crest and his pilot repelled challenge after challenge up the straight to record this sensational seven-timer. The crowd went berserk, and even TV's *Grandstand* held back *Final Score* until after the race. Original odds for the

seven-timer were in the region of 25,095/1.

Dettori however, experienced the other side of life in 2000 when involved in a horrific plane crash at Newmarket. His great friend Ray Cochrane saved Frankie's life and he recovered fully.

Riding still for Godolphin, Dettori has added a host of big-race triumphs to his collection with Swain, Sakhee, Marienbard, Kazzia, Daylami and many more. He remains a world-class jockey, a great ambassador for racing and hugely popular with the people.

BELOW Dettori and Vintage Tipple land the Darley Irish Oaks Race run at the Curragh Racecourse in 2003

Dickinson

BORN IN 1950, MICHAEL DICKINSON started riding in the point-to-point world and became champion amateur in the 1969-70 season. He then turned professional and won 378 races. His father Tony held the license and, aided by his talented wife Monica, the Dickinsons became a highly successful family outfit.

In 1980 he took over the training establishment at Harwood in Yorkshire and sent out his first winner when Murray's Gift won for him at Ludlow in October.

RIGHT Michael Dickinson at Churchill Downs with Tapit

BELOW Michael Dickinson in 2004

He had ridden five Cheltenham Festival winners as a jockey and took little time leaving his mark as a trainer there with wins with Rathgorman in the Champion Chase and Silver Buck in the Gold Cup, where he also saddled the second, Bregawn.

Dickinson continued to mop up jumping's major prizes, winning the King George VI three times with Silver Buck in 1980 and Wayward Lad (1982, 1983). He saddled Badsworth Boy to win the Queen Mother Champion Chase twice (1983 and 1984) to add to Rathgorman's success. He won the Trainers' Championship three times from 1981-84.

On 12 December 1982 Dickinson set a world record of 12 winners in one day, but his finest hour was to come in 1983 when he achieved what many believe to be the greatest training feat in saddling the first five home in the Cheltenham Gold Cup. Bregawn won the race, ridden by Graham Bradley, followed by Captain John, Wayward Lad, Silver Buck and Ashley House. This achievement was unprecedented.

A year later Dickinson gave up his jumping career to become private trainer to Robert Sangster at Manton in Wiltshire, training flat horses. The venture was not a success and in 1987 he went to Maryland in America where he enjoyed greater luck, winning the Breeders' Cup Mile with Da Hoss in 1996 and 1998.

Dunwoody

BORN INTO A RACING FAMILY IN Belfast, Northern Ireland in 1964, Richard Dunwoody quickly established himself at the forefront of National Hunt racing. His most prolific partnership was with Desert Orchid, on whom he won seven races.

His first winner was on Game Trust at Cheltenham in 1983 and he went on to win the Grand National on West Tip (1986), the Champion Hurdle and the Cheltenham Gold Cup on Charter Party (1988). He also won the Champion Hurdle in 1990 on Kribensis and the National in 1994 on Minnehoma, and was declared Champion Jockey no less than three times.

Sadly, an arm injury forced 'the Prince' (as he was dubbed by his fellow jockeys) to quit racing in December 1999, the same year he beat Peter Scudamore's record of all-time winners, having ridden 1,699 in Britain. He went on to become a racing pundit for the BBC, newspaper columnist and public speaker, as well as running his own sports marketing business.

In 2001, Richard was voted Champion of Champions. Former Champion Jockey and fellow pundit John Francome paid him a handsome compliment when he said: 'He made bad horses look good and every day he was at his best.' Dunwoody was awarded the MBE in June 1993 and his autobiography was published in 2000.

BELOW Dunwoody on Paddy's Return after winning at Cheltenham in 1996

Earth Summit

RIGHT Earth Summit in training at Naunton in Gloucester in 1999
BELOW Earth Summit jumping a fence on his way to victory at the 1998 Grand National

EARTH SUMMIT WAS FOALED IN 1988. A bay gelding by Celtic Cone out of Win Green Hill, he was bought by former Champion Jockey Peter Scudamore to run for a six-strong partnership.

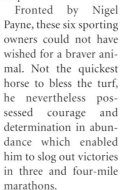

Fronted by Nigel Payne, these six sporting owners could not have wished for a braver animal. Not the quickest horse to bless the turf, he nevertheless possessed courage and determination in abundance which enabled him to slog out victories in three and four-mile marathons.

Trained at Naunton, Cheltenham, by Nigel Twiston-Davies, Earth Summit is still the only horse to have completed the National treble, namely the Scottish, Welsh and Aintree Grand Nationals.

He won his Scottish National in 1994 along with the Steel Plate and Sections Young Chasers final. In 1995 he won Peter Marsh Chase before a life-threatening injury kept him out of racing for sixteen months. Twiston-Davies brought him back to racing after some skilful handling and won the Welsh National in 1997.

Then all eyes turned to Aintree where Carl Llewellyn took over from the injured Tom Jenks and won the National on atrocious ground. Earth Summit retired in 2000, having won over £400,000 in prize money, to be looked after by Marcella Bayliss who had been his lass throughout his racing days.

Eclipse

BRED FOR THE DUKE of Cumberland on his estate at Windsor in 1764, Eclipse – by Marske out of the mare Spiletta and named after the astronomical event that occurred that year – was probably one of the most important horses in racing.

In all about 98% of modern thoroughbreds are descended from him. He was bought originally by William Wildman but was then sold on to famous gambler Denis O'Kelly.

ABOVE Eclipse pictured at Newmarket by painter George Stubbs

Eclipse ran his first race in 1769, at the age of five and was an impressive winner at Epsom. Over the next two years he ran a total of 18 races in which he was never headed or even stretched. He was a strong animal and jockeys had a hard job to hold him; such was his superiority that he was never whipped or spurred. However, such was his dominance at that time that much of the opposition were scared off and eight of his victories were walkovers.

He retired to stud in 1771 where he sired 335 winners including Pot-8-O's who was responsible in time for the top-class thoroughbreds Hyperion, Kelso and Sea Bird. Eclipse died in 1789 at the age of 35 from a bout of colic.

Eddery

WITH MORE THAN 4,000 CAREER victories and 11 times a Champion Jockey, Pat Eddery can only be described as one of the finest jockeys in modern racing history. His success was not limited to English Classics and in 1999 he broke Lester Piggott's record of 465 Group winners.

He began his racing career as apprentice to Frenchie Nicholson and he rode his first winner, Alvaro, at Epsom in 1968. Three years later he became the UK's Champion Apprentice. In a further three years he was to clinch his first full title riding for Peter Walwyn.

He stayed with Walwyn throughout the 1970s where he partnered more than 800 winners, Including the Derby and King George V & Queen Elizabeth Stakes on Grundy in 1975, but in 1980 he collaborated with trainer Vincent O'Brien before moving on to K Abdullah and finally becoming freelance. Highspots in that decade included a Derby win on Golden Fleece (1980) and the Prix de l'Arc on Detroit (1982)

Since partnering Bosra Sham to victory in the 1,000 Guineas in 1996, Eddery

TOP Eddery riding With Iris at Newbury in 1999

RIGHT A relaxed Pat Eddery at Goodwood in 1994

BELOW Eddery after his last race, at Doncaster, before retiring in 2003

has ridden a winner in every Classic where his skills in the saddle have been demonstrated time and again. These were especially illustrated in the 1986 Prix de L'Arc de Triomphe while riding the legendary Dancing Brave, where he emerged victorious against a field of no less than seven Group One-winning horses.

Endurance

IN STEEPLECHASING TERMS, THE Grand National is regarded as an endurance event, given its distance, but those involved in true endurance racing would view the race as a bit of a stroll.

Distances covered in these gruelling, often international events will generally be above 25 miles and can reach 275 for a multi-day extravaganza. The sport is very popular in the United

Arab Emirates, with the home-bred Arab horses, produced from lines going back hundreds of years, being the most suitable to tackle the often inhospitable terrain. The UAE teams are highly organised and, for extended events, will often have a backup team similar to those used in rallying or the Tour de France. When international events take place, UAE riders can always be guaranteed to be amongst the prizes.

In the United States, the sport often takes place in the wide-open spaces of states like Utah with its spectacular scenery. If you haven't got your own horse, the authorities will sometimes supply one.

In Britain, Endurance GB stages over one hundred events a year and arranges for training at all levels.

ABOVE A dramatic close-up of a competitor in the 2001 Tevis Cup Ride in the Sierra Mountains, USA

LEFT Riders passing through Stump Cross Caverns during the Sunday Telegraph Golden Horseshoe 60-mile ride in 1966

Fallon

BORN ON 22 FEBRUARY 1965 in Crusheen, County Clare, Kieron Fallon embarked on a racing career at 17 and, serving his apprenticeship with Kevin Prendergast, rode his first winner in June 1984 at Navan.

In 1988 he tried his luck in England, and Jimmy Fitzgerald at Malton was instrumental in helping him in his career. Staying in the north, he began riding for Lynda Ramsden in 1993 and made a big impression for this shrewd yard.

Henry Cecil signed Fallon as stable jockey in 1996 and he enjoyed great success with the Newmarket trainer, becoming Champion Jockey in 1997 and winning his first two Classics with Sleepytime (1,000 Guineas) and Reams of Verse (Oaks). A Derby (Oath, 1999), Oaks (Ramruma, 1999) and a 1,000 Guineas (Wince, 1999) followed, as did two more Championships, before Fallon joined Sir Michael Stoute in 2000.

Another highly successful period followed, winning the Championship from 2002-04. Classics came Fallon's way with Golan (2,000 Guineas, 2001), Russian Rhythm (1,000 Guineas, 2003), Ouija Board (Oaks, 2004) and two English Derbys with Kris Kin (2003) and North Light (2004).

Fallon had a great year in 2003, winning eight Group One races and the Breeders' Cup Filly and Mare Turf with Islington. A year later he won the same race with the ultra-consistent Ouija Board. But Frankie Dettori took the

Jockey's title from him in 2004.

The following year saw him link up with Aidan O'Brien, making it a winning combination when he won the 2,000 and 1,000 Guineas on Footsteps inthesand and Virginia Waters respectively and the Irish Derby in the colours of Michael Tabor with Hurricane Run. Other Group races followed with Oratorio and Scorpion. Then in October, in Paris, he won the Prix de L'Arc de Triomphe with Hurricane Run.

A strong, wilful rider in perfect rhythm with his mount, Fallon is a shrewd judge whose knack is to be in the right place at the right time.

Flat

THE BRITISH FLAT-racing season traditionally runs from March to November but year-round racing is now possible with the advent of all-weather tracks.

The main action takes place during those summer months when all major meetings take place and the Classic races are run. These are the 1,000 Guineas and 2,000 Guineas run at Newmarket, the Oaks and Derby taking place at Epsom and the St Leger, the oldest race amongst them, at Doncaster.

Countless meetings are held throughout the year, with the high spots coming at the Epsom Derby meeting, Royal Ascot and Goodwood which comes with a 'glorious' tag. Of course many other high-class events take place which also attract the best in the sport.

Jockeys compete for the much-coveted Jockeys Championship, trainers vie for the leading trainer title and owners are always pleased to be ahead on the prize money. In addition the apprentice jockeys keenly battle for their own Championship, which is desperately competitive (in 2005 there was a tie).

Before the season starts, much hype emerges from the various stables as to how well their horses are likely to run. Some deliver the goods, whilst others remain as also-rans.

Francis

BORN RICHARD STANLEY FRANCIS in South Wales on 31 October 1920, Dick Francis was the son of a jockey who went on to have a successful career as a jockey himself, winning more than 350 races.

During the Second World War he served in the Royal Air Force as a Spitfire pilot before leaving in 1946 and starting a new career in horseracing. He was jockey to the late Queen Mother between 1953 and 1957 before being forced to retire due to a serious injury after a fall. His most famous moment came in the 1956 Grand National riding Devon Loch, owned by the Queen Mother, who collapsed on the run-in only yards from the winning post

In 1957 he published his first book and autobiography, *The Sport of Queens*. He became racing correspondent for 16 years on the *Sunday Express*, and became a successful fiction writer when he published his first novel, *Dead Cert*, in 1962. He has written a book every year, except in 1998, for more than 30 years. The plots centre around the horseracing world.

Dick's late wife Mary was instrumental in the research and editing for his books. His latest novel *Under Orders* will be published in hardback in September 2006. Dick Francis was made an Officer of the Order of the British Empire in 1984.

BELOW Dick Francis with one of his novels in 1988

Francome

FROM HUMBLE BEGINNINGS, John Francome went on to become a successful jockey and trainer and one of the foremost figures of all time in the racing world.

Born in a Swindon council house on 13 December 1952, he left school with few qualifications and a childhood ambition to play football for his home-town team. This did not materialise.

The Francomes had no connections with horses and no funds to compete with the racing set, but a ride on a donkey at the age of six had the youngster hooked on horses and riding. He persuaded his parents to buy him a pony which he named Black Beauty.

Unusually for a jockey his first successes were as a show-jumper. In his autobiography *Born Lucky,* published in 1985, he merely gives winning a gold medal at the 1969 European Show-Jumping Championships with the Great Britain team one line. He realised that show-jumping offered lit-

RIGHT Francome jumps Wayward Lass in 1983

BELOW Now retired from racing, John Francome enjoys playing golf

tle financial security and remarked: 'To become a jockey suddenly seemed the natural solution.'

The move from show-jumping to National Hunt proved no problem and his career as a jockey began as an apprentice with trainer Fred Winter in 1969. As an apprentice jockey, he won on Multygrey for Godfrey Burr at Worcester later that same year and took over from Richard Pitman as first jockey in 1972. Six years later, he won the Cheltenham Gold Cup on Midnight Court and the Champion Hurdle on Sea Pigeon in 1981. Francome won the Champion Jockey title

seven times between 1975 and 1985.

Other famous mounts include Brown Chamberlain and Burrough Hill Lad. He retired from racing after 1,138 winners in Britain, the final win taking place with Gamblers Cup at Huntingdon in April 1985. His decision was made after falling at Chepstow and being trodden on by the Reject.

Francome spent 18 months as a trainer before joining Channel 4 TV's racing team in 1987. He has since become a successful broadcaster and novelist. Dead Weight was the 19th book he has written since his autobiography, and he has made it onto the Top 100 list of most borrowed authors from UK libraries. Although he still enjoys football, John Francome's other hobbies include tennis, golf and music. He is a noted after-dinner speaker and was awarded the MBE in 1986.

Godolphin

ABOVE Godolphin trainer, Saeed bin Suroor, at Ascot in 2004

RIGHT Sheikh Mohammed at the Dubai World Cup in 2005

THE GODOLPHIN ORGANISATION is a modern racing phenomenon which has achieved an enormous amount of success in a very short space of time.

Starting in 1992 with only a small group of horses, Godolphin now has countless animals in training. This is monitored by the watchful eye of His Highness Sheikh Mohammed bin Rashid Al Maktoum, a man who believes in big being beautiful.

During the winter months Godolphin horses are based at the Al Quoz stables in Dubai, where horses are both rested after the rigours of the European season and prepared for the Dubai International Racing Carnival, an annual event running from January to March.

In the summer, the horses are transported to England where they are housed at either the Godolphin Stables or Moulton Paddocks in Newmarket, a base for all international commitments.

With its enormous buying power and private stud facilities, the stable only deals in the highest quality animals, a fact reflected in a record of over 125 top-level winners on the world stage.

Amongst these elite horses was the late Dubai Millennium, a wonderful creature regarded by some as the greatest horse in the world, partnered by Frankie Dettori.

Golden Miller

OWNED BY THE ECCENtric Dorothy Paget, Golden Miller won the first of his five Cheltenham Gold Cups in 1932 with Ted Leader in the saddle. Little was made of the result as both the leading fancies for the race had failed to complete. Then a year later Golden Miller took the crown again, winning his fifth consecutive race that season.

ABOVE Golden Miller in 1935

In 1934 he completed an amazing and unique double by winning the Cheltenham Gold Cup by six lengths and the Grand National in record time with Gerry Wilson as jockey. His trainer Basil Briscoe then aimed Golden Miller at the 1935 National, using the Gold Cup as a prep race. Watched by a large crowd, he won in a record time after a hard fought battle from the final fence with Thomond II. But though he started favourite for the National he failed to repeat his victory of the previous year.

1936 saw Golden Miller win his fifth Gold Cup and, after the abandonment of the race in 1937, he finished a gallant second the following year to Morse Code.

In all, Golden Miller won 28 of his 52 races. He was trained for the majority of his career by Basil Briscoe, but later by Donald Snow and Owen Anthony. 17 different jockeys had the pleasure to ride this remarkable Irish-bred chaser before he died at the age of 30. A statue of Golden Miller was erected at Cheltenham in 1989.

Grand National

FIRST RUN IN 1839 UNDER THE TITLE of the Grand Liverpool Steeple Chase and won by the aptly-named Lottery, the Grand National holds a unique place in National Hunt racing. (Renamed in 1843 as the Liverpool and National Steeple Chase, it took up its present title of Grand National Steeple Chase in 1847.)

The race, run over four and a half miles at Aintree, is a true test of horse and jockey with 30 fences to jump, an added complication being that they are higher on the take-off side than on the landing side. Becher's Brook, named after a rider, Captain Becher, who fell into the brook, and the Chair are two of the most formidable obstacles.

BELOW The Grand National Trophy

The fascination with the race is such that it is watched by over 600 million viewers around the world and rarely are they let down in terms of drama. In 1928, a year after the first radio broadcast of the race, Easter Hero found himself straddled across the Canal Turn fence; 20 runners were taken out in one go. 1967 saw a similar incident when the appropriately named Popham Down caused a pile-up at the 23rd fence. Foinavon, at 100/1 the race's longest-priced winner to date, had been so far behind he missed the initial fracas and sailed over the fence without trouble to win for rider John Buckingham.

In 1956, the Queen Mother's Devon Loch was running well clear to the winning line before inexplicably falling on the flat, leaving ESB to run through and take the prize. Esha Ness was famously first past the post in 'the race that never was' in 1993; half of the jockeys had not

realised there was a false start and completed the race only to find it declared void. Four years later in 1997 the course had to be evacuated due to a bomb scare and the race run on the Monday instead of the Saturday; Lord Gyllene was the eventual winner.

Merryman won the first televised National in 1960, while the following year Nicholas Silver became only the second grey to win following The Lamb's victory in 1869.

Although no female jockey has yet won the race, Charlotte Brew became the first to take part in 1977 and Geraldine Rees, riding Cheers in 1982, was the first to complete the course.

Great stories surround this unique race in 1981 when Bob Champion fought back from cancer to capture the prize on Aldaniti who had himself fought back from career-threatening injuries. And who can forget the brilliant Red Rum who, trained on the beach at Southport by Ginger McCain, became the only horse to win it three times?

ABOVE The start of the 2003 Grand National, with the Aintree grandstand in the background

Handicapping

BEARING IN MIND that close to half of the races run in Britain are designated as handicaps, the handicapping system is central to the administration of horseracing.

In basic terms, a handicap is a race where all the runners are allotted weight, allocated against their record and ability, which theoretically gives them all an equal chance of victory. A total of ten handicappers, employed by the British Horseracing Board, are allotted the task of striking this sensible balance. All handicap statistics are retained by racing administrators Weatherbys.

In flat racing, a horse generally has had to run three times before it is eligible for a handicap which at least gives some indication of form, The handicapper will often make his assessment based on performances against other horses. A run of wins will almost certainly lead to a hike up the weights and a sequence of losses means the opposite.

As a rule, the horse deemed to be the best runner in any handicap will carry top weight, with the lesser lights taking order down a diminishing scale. Some horses perform carrying any amount of substantial weight, while others simply find it difficult to handle extra loads.

High Chaparral

FOALED IN 1999, THIS BAY COLT BY Sadlers Well's out of Kasora won the admiration of the public with his consistency and his courage. Owned by Michael Tabor and Sue Magnier and trained at Ballydoyle by Aidan O'Brien, High Chaparral gave an indication of what was to come when winning the *Racing Post* Trophy as a two year-old.

He wintered well and the following season took the Leopardstown Derby trial en route to a crack at the Epsom Derby. With Johnny Murtagh in the saddle, he beat his stablemate Hawk Wing in a close finish. Then, with Mick Kinane back on board, he took the Irish Derby by four lengths at the odds of 1/3, from 200/1 outsider Sholokhov. A trip to America that season ended with a victory in the Breeders' Cup to follow his third place in the Prix de L'Arc.

Instead of retiring to stud duties, High Chaparral was campaigned again as a four year-old, winning the Royal Whip and Irish Champion Stakes and achieving another third place in the Prix de L'Arc, before returning to America for the Breeder Cup Turf at Santa Anita. It was here that he showed his guts and determination to dead-heat with the American-trained Johar. The epic battle, with the pair finishing in front of High Chaparral's old rival Falbrav, proved a fitting race to bow out on.

ABOVE High Chaparral with Kevin Darley after landing The Racing Post trophy at Doncaster in 2001

LEFT A Vanity Fair cartoon of Major E H Eggerton, official handicapper to the Jockey Club in 1889

Hurdling

NATIONAL HUNT (SEE ENTRY FOR more details) rules apply to jump racing, which can broadly be divided into hurdling and steeplechases. Hurdling is run over distances of two to three and a half miles over smaller, less rigid (although at least three and a half feet high) fences and horses are not allowed to run until 1 July in the year in which they reach three years old.

Cheltenham is the home of National Hunt racing, of which hurdling is a major part. The first day of the Cheltenham Festival features the Champion Hurdle. This grade one event is run over two miles and half a furlong and has been dominated by Irish racers for the past decade.

RIGHT Be prepared to take a tumble when hurdling…

BELOW Jumping a hurdle at Sandown in 2005

Aiden O'Brien trained Irish legend Istabraq, one of only five horses to win the Champion Hurdle three times. Sired by Sadler's Wells, Istabraq won two of his 11 races on the flat for John Gosden. John Durkan, Gosden's assistant, persuaded JP McManus to buy the horse and send him hurdling. In 1998, Istabraq won the Champion Hurdle by 12 lengths, the biggest margin for 66 years. He also won 23 of his 29 races over hurdles.

The final day at Cheltenham sees the grade one Triumph Hurdle. The race is run over two miles and one furlong and is often described as a cavalry charge. The race attracts many riders and as a novice event there are many inexperienced horses in the running so a fair amount of luck is required for horse and rider to do well.

Ireland

ABOVE The scenic Curragh racecourse in County Kildare

IRELAND, THE THIRD LARGEST island in Europe, began its love affair with horseracing in the mid 18th Century. The first recorded steeplechase took place in County Cork in 1752.

The steeplechase evolved from the European pastime of foxhunting, of which both the Irish and English were enthusiastic. The first courses were often over rough terrain which meant that horse and rider were forced to deal with whatever unforeseen obstacles might be in their path. As the sport progressed, the basic steeplechase course evolved into a pre-determined route with a set length and reasonable hurdles.

Today, racing in Ireland is organised like a tour, where different racecourses are used every weekend. National Hunt racing is more popular in Ireland with jump meetings taking place all year round. Courses range from 280 acres at Limerick's Greenmount Park to smaller affairs like Sligo with just 56 acres. Top racing takes place at Leopardstown and the Curragh, but the lower-class courses are no less spectacular and ensure that racing reaches the masses.

There is also a great deal of variety in Irish racing. At Laytown, for example, a temporary course is set up over the beach during low-tide so that horses sprint over the flat wet sand.

For many years, Irish horses have performed well at Cheltenham and, every March, a significant number of Irish race-goers attend the four-day Festival. They were delighted when, on 17 March 2006, War of Attrition, ridden by Conor O'Dwyer, trained by Mouse Morris and owned by Michael O'Leary, won the Gold Cup on St Patrick's Day.

Istabraq

FOALED IN 1992, THIS BAY GELDING by Sadlers Wells was originally owned by Hamdan Al Maktoum. His flat career was nothing extraordinary and it would be fair to say that, although he won two races at three, he was probably a disappointment to his trainer John Gosden. Not many would have envisaged the impact Istabraq would make when sent hurdling.

Assistant trainer for John Gosden was John Durkan, about to set up as a trainer himself who, persuaded Irish owner JP McManus to buy the horse, but tragically Durkan, after being diagnosed with leukemia, was unable to take up the training task. The horse went to Aidan O'Brien where he was handled with the utmost skill.

In 1997 Istabraq won the Sun Alliance Novices Hurdle at Cheltenham, proving John Durkan right. Then a year later ridden by regular pilot Charlie Swan he won his first Champion Hurdle. A quick and accurate jumper, he then went on to win the Champion Hurdle at Cheltenham in 1999 and 2000 to make it a hat-trick in tremendous

ABOVE Charlie Swan and Istabraq power up the hill at Cheltenham to land the 2000 Smurfit Champion Hurdle Race

RIGHT Swan on his way to victory in the Champion Hurdle on Istabraq in 1999

style. Not content with that, in the same period he won the Irish Champion Hurdle three times.

2001 saw Istabraq win the Irish Champion Hurdle for a fourth time, but the outbreak of foot and mouth in this year thwarted a fourth attempt at Cheltenham. Istabraq retired after being pulled up in the 2002 Champion Hurdle, a victor in 23 of his 29 starts and accumulating over a million pounds in prize money.

Jockey Club

AROUND 1750, RICH AND influential men used to meet at the Star and Garter public house in Pall Mall, London, to share their interest in racing. The gathering was intended to promote fellowship between breeders and racing people and culminated in the Jockey Club being formed.

The Club quickly acquired authority and prestige, eventually becoming the governing body of racing. Two years later, the Jockey Club leased a plot of land in Newmarket where 'The Coffee Room' was constructed as a meeting-place for members. On expiry of the lease, the Club bought the freehold and new buildings were added to the original site. Professor Sir Albert Richardson, sometime President of the Royal Academy redesigned the buildings during the mid 1930s.

Until April 2006, the Jockey Club was responsible for the day-to-day regulation of UK horseracing and – together with the British Horseracing Board and the Horserace Betting Levy Board – provided management for horseracing. Regulatory responsibility was transferred to a new Horseracing Regulatory Authority from 3 April.

ABOVE The Jockey Club's impressive Newmarket premises

BELOW Strictly members only!

Jockey Club Estates (JCE) is the Jockey Club's property and land management company responsible for the management and administration of 4,500 acres of land in and around Newmarket. The Rowley Mile and July racecourses are included in the property portfolio along with the National Stud land and the National Horseracing Museum. The company's primary role is the management and development of the facilities for the training of thoroughbred racehorses. In addition to the Newmarket gallops, in 2006 Jockey Club Estates purchased 500 acres of training grounds in Lambourn.

Racing Welfare, a registered charity, is a company limited by guarantee which has the Jockey Club as its sole trustee. It was formed in 2001 by the amalgamation of three racing charities, namely the Stable Lads' Welfare Trust, the Jockey Club Charitable Trust and the Racing Welfare Charities. Racing Welfare is the only charity to offer help to the 60,000 people working in the racing industry today. The charity provides support to those injured or disabled, plus education, information and advice, financial support and affordable housing for those who retire.

The Jockey Club is still dedicated to improving the sport and investing in its future. It seeks to support the long-term interests of racing and continues to own and manage 13 racecourses through Racecourse Holdings Trust (RHT) – a subsidiary of the Jockey Club – which focuses on maximising cashflow from the operation and management of racecourses. Money is reinvested to develop the quality of flat and jump racing.

Johnson

DESPITE HIS FAMILY HAVING NO previous connection with horseracing, David Johnson is one of the sport's most prolific National Hunt owners. With an exceptional working relationship with Martin Pipe, his regular trainer and whom he highly respects, Johnson built a successful owner and trainer team.

David Johnson's father worked at the docks in London's East End, but he himself became a successful businessman and financier, running his own company before he decided to become involved in horseracing. Initially he bought flat-course racehorses, his first winner being Café Noir at Folkestone. However, his best flat-course racehorse was Mister Majestic, which won the Middle Park Stakes in 1986 at Newmarket.

Later, he began to concentrate on jump racing, in which he has enjoyed numerous successes. He has been Champion Jump Owner four times and maintained the title for three consecutive seasons. He has won the Thomas Pink Gold Cup at Cheltenham on three occasions with Challenger du Luc, 1996; Cyfor Malta, 1998 and Lady Cricket, 2000. He also won the 2002 Hennessy Cognac Gold Cup with Take Control while another of his horses, Wahiba Sands, was one of only five horses to beat Best Mate by winning the First National Gold Cup in 2001. Jockey Timmy Murphy is a regular partner for his horses.

ABOVE Jockey Tony McCoy with the Johnson owned 'The Real Bandit', 2003

King George VI & Queen Elizabeth Diamond Stakes

KING GEORGE VI & QUEEN ELIZABETH DIAMOND STAKES

RIGHT Nijinsky is led in by his trainer Vincent O'Brien after Lester Piggott rode him to victory in the 1970 King George VI & Queen Elizabeth II Stakes at Ascot

OPPOSITE Prince Aly Khan leading in his father's horse, Tulyar, which had just won the 1952 King George VI & Queen Elizabeth Stakes

FIRST RUN IN 1951 OVER 1½ miles at Ascot, when named King George VI & Queen Elizabeth Festival of Britain Stakes, this race has been won by a host of truly great horses. Run in July of each year it is recognised along with the Prix de L'Arc de Triumphe as the most important weight-for-age race in Europe.

It has drawn opposition from all over the world and, as early as 1955, the prize was

wrested from these shores by the French-trained Vimy. In fact the French made quite a habit of winning it in the late 1950s and early 1960s, and in 1956 the unbeaten Ribot from Italy left his mark with a three-length victory.

After the Derby at Epsom in June, the winner often heads to the King George VI & Queen Elizabeth Diamond Stakes to test himself against the top horses from a year or so before. The 1970s threw up three top three year-olds from 1970-72 in Nijinsky, Mill Reef and Brigadier Gerard, and a contest in 1975 that is still talked about as the 'Race of the Century' where Grundy and Bustino battled like tigers inside the final furlong for the younger Grundy to win by half a length in record time.

Other notable winners have been Shergar (1981), Dancing Brave (1983), Nashwan (1986), Lammtarra (1992), Daylami (1999) and Monjeu (2000).

Although the name of the race has changed twice, being known as the King George VI & Queen Elizabeth Stakes from 1952 until 1974 when Diamond was added to the name, the supreme quality of one of the turf's most prestigious races remains.

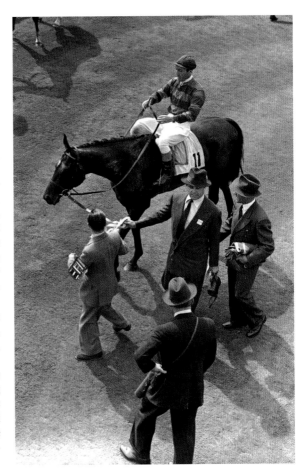

Kentucky Derby

HELD AT CHURCHILL DOWNS, Louisville, Kentucky, and run on the first Saturday in May, the Derby forms the first leg of the American Triple Crown. First staged in 1875, it was originally over a distance, like the English Derby, of a mile and a half until 1896 when it was run, as today, over a mile and a quarter.

This race for three year-olds is steeped in tradition and is also known as the 'Run for the Roses', as the winner receives a blanket of red roses. Crowds of over 150,000 are regularly drawn to the race where, as the horses parade before the race, they can be found standing and singing 'My Old Kentucky Home' while consuming the traditional Mint Julep, a mixture of Bourbon, mint and sugar syrup.

Unlike the English Derby geldings are allowed to compete alongside colts and fillies, carrying a weight along with the colts of nine stone and the fillies of eight stone nine pounds. The idea of the race

RIGHT Action at the 1988 Kentucky Derby, with the impressive Churchill Downs grandstand in the background

BELOW Crowds enjoying the sunshine at the 1988 Kentucky Derby

was conceived by Colonel M Lewis Clark after visiting Europe and watching the English Derby and France's Grand Prix de Paris, later to become the Prix de L'Arc de Triomphe.

Many great horses have won this race, but to go on and win the Triple Crown – completed by the Preakness Stakes, run in Baltimore, and the Belmont Stakes in New York – is a difficult task. Notable horses to achieve this include War Admiral, Citation, Secretariat, Seattle Slew and Affirmed.

Langtry

THE TURF'S HISTORY IS CRAMMED full of colourful and extremely interesting characters. Lillie Langtry was one such person. Born in Jersey on 13 October 1853, it was not long before she made a favourable impression, receiving her first marriage proposal at the age of 14.

She declined, but in 1874, aged 20, married Edward Langtry. Just three years later she began her affair with the Prince of Wales, later to become Edward VII, who bought her a 'love nest' in Bournemouth. After being presented at Court to Queen Victoria in 1878, she became the Prince's official mistress and was escorted to all social events including Ascot and Goodwood Races.

The Prince was a keen race-goer and eventually won the Derby three times with Persimmon (1896), Diamond Jubilee (1900) and Minoru, when Edward VII in 1909.

1881 saw the secret birth of Lillie's daughter in Paris and in that same year she made her first appearance on stage. She became enormously popular in fashionable society and in 1882 toured America with her own theatre company. Six years later she returned, now divorced from her husband.

On buying her first racehorse, Lillie Langtry registered as an owner under the name of Mr Jersey as, under Jockey Club rules, women could not be owners. She owned training stables at Etheldreda House in Newmarket and was a successful owner, winning the Ascot Gold Cup, the Cesarewitch, Goodwood Cup and Jockey Club Cup with Merman.

Lillie Langtry died in Monaco in 1929.

ABOVE The legendary Lillie Langtry at Newbury Racecourse in 1909

Legends

WHAT MAKES A LEGEND OF THE turf? Many great horses have their own entries in this book, but here we spotlight a few who were perhaps unlucky to miss the cut.

Phar Lap was foaled in 1926. Unfashionably bred by a sire who failed to win a race in England, and a dam who was unplaced on her only start. This did not stop him from becoming a National hero in Australia, although the start to his racing career was unimpressive, losing nine of his first ten races. In the 1929-30 season as a three-year-old, he started to get the message and won the AJC and Victoria Derbys and then went on to win his last nine races that season.

In 1930-31 Phar Lap ran up a sequence of fourteen wins in succession including the Melbourne Cup, and winning his first eight races as a five year-old. Then in 1932 Phar Lap arrived in America to contest the world's richest race in the ten-furlong Agua Caliente Handicap which he won for trainer Harry Telford.

He also won his next race decisively and it was suggested he was the greatest horse to race in North America. After the race he fell ill and died; some say he was poisoned. Phar Lap won 37 of his 51 races.

Man O War foaled in 1917 was

RIGHT Ribot is congratulated by Incisa della Rochetta, the owner's daughter, after winning the 1956 Prix de L'Arc de Triomphe

BELOW Phar Lap riden by Jim Pike in 1929

trained by Louis Feustel in America and, by winning 20 of his 21 races, was regarded as America's greatest champion. In his career he set five American records before going to stud where he became a successful stallion. 'Big Red', as he was known, died in 1947.

Italy had their own wonder horse with the unbeaten Ribot in the 1950s. His winning run was attained over distances from five furlongs to a mile and seven furlongs and included two Prix de L'Arc de Triomphe victories (1955-56), by wide margins, and a King George VI & Queen Elizabeth Stakes (1956) by five lengths. A winner of sixteen races, he retired to stud where he became champion sire three times.

Longchamp

THE PRESTIGIOUS COURSE at Longchamp is situated in the fashionable Paris district of the Bois de Boulogne, the land having been acquired for horseracing via a lease signed in 1856. The first ever meeting took place the following year on 27 April, where the huge crowd were delighted by the presence of Napoleon III, his wife Eugenie and other assorted royals.

The five-race card featured a horse called Miss Gladiator whose statue stands at the track's main entrance to this day. That opening event firmly put Longchamp on the map and established the location as somewhere for the upper classes to be seen.

The course continued to be popular over subsequent decades but closed during World War I, only to re-open and stage the first running of the famous Prix de L'Arc de Triomphe in 1920. This race has long been regarded as one of the world's finest and the 'Arc'

RIGHT Fashionable race-goers at Longchamp in 1914

BELOW Johnny Murtagh riding Sinndar crosses the finish line during the Group One Prix de l'Arc de Triomphe at Longchamp in 2000

weekend attracts racegoers from far and wide. To win at Longchamp at any level is regarded as a triumph and riders from Britain take great pleasure in running off with the major prizes.

One of the location's features is a unique windmill, once part of a monastery dating back to 1256.

Magnier

JOHN MAGNIER WAS BORN IN 1948, the son of an Irish stud farm owner. Leaving school at 15, he helped run the family business on the death of his father. He steadily built up his bloodstock business and, with trainer Vincent O'Brien (also his father-in-law on his marriage to Sue O'Brien), propelled Coolmore Stud into the big league.

With pools heir and racehorse owner Robert Sangster alongside them, top thoroughbreds were bought from the United States. The stock was raced in England and Ireland to advertise their potential before breeding from them. There was no tax on profits made from bloodstock in Ireland and Magnier and the Coolmore Mafia, as they are nicknamed, were in a powerful and lucrative position.

Magnier bought well and, on the retirement of Vincent O'Brien, Aiden O'Brien (no relation) took over the reins at Ballydoyle. With owners such as Michael Tabor joining forces, Sue Magnier's colours of dark blue have been seen on all major prizes. High Chaparral, Hawk Wing, Galileo, King of Kings, Footsteps in the Sand, Virginia Waters, Giants Causeway and Rock of Gibraltar have taken Group One races in Britain and abroad on a regular basis.

But it was with Rock of Gibraltar that Magnier hit the headlines regarding his dispute with Manchester United manager Sir Alex Ferguson. The horse, who went on to win the 2002, 2,000 Guineas and six other Group One races, took £1.1 million in prize money, but Sir Alex (in whose colours it ran) felt he should receive half of the colt's earnings at stud. Eventually an out-of-court agreement was made.

With an estimated wealth of over £200 million, John Magnier remains publicity-shy, shrewd and ahead of the game.

ABOVE Magnier's Rock of Gibraltar with PJ Coldville, in training at Arlington Park

BELOW John Magnier receives the Horse of the Year Award for Hurricane Run in 2005

McCoy

OPPOSITE Tony McCoy at Cheltenham in 2004

RIGHT McCoy and Bongo Fury clear the second last flight to win the Mares Handicap Hurdle Race at Sandown in 2005

BELOW McCoy and Rubberdubber clear the last fence before landing the Vodafone Novices Handicap Steeplechase at Newbury in 2006

NICKNAMED AP, ANTHONY PETER McCoy is widely regarded as the greatest jump jockey ever. Born on 4 May 1974 in Moneyglass, County Antrim, Northern Ireland, McCoy rode his first winner at Thurles in March 1992 on Legal Steps. Success in Ireland led him to England two years later and success at Exeter in September 1994 set him on his way to a record 74 wins in that season. He has since gone from strength to strength and been Champion Jockey nine times since 1995-96.

McCoy set a new National Hunt record of 253 winners in a season and the fastest jockey to reach the 1,000th winner mark on Majadou at Cheltenham in December 1999. He became rode his 1,500th winner on Celtic Native at Exeter in December 2001 and beat Sir Gordon Richards' record of 269 winners in a season for all types of racing the following April; Valfonic at Warwick giving him a total of 289 wins.

He spent much of his career riding for Martin Pipe but is now retained by Irish millionaire and avid horse owner JP McManus and normally rides for ex-jockey Jonjo O'Neill's Jackdaw's Castle stable. He can be seen on the racecourse sporting a green and gold-hooped jersey and white cap. What is amazing about McCoy is that he is exceptionally tall at five foot 10 inches and heavy (10 stone six pounds) for a jockey, yet his ability is unquestionable.

His victory at Uttoxeter in August 2002 on Mighty Mantefalco saw his achievements soar when he surpassed Richard Dunwoody's record to become the leading jumps rider of all time. In January 2004, Tony McCoy rode his 2,000th winner when riding Magical Bailiwick to victory at Wincanton.

Despite winning both the Cheltenham

Gold Cup (Mr Mulligan in 1997) and the Champion Hurdle twice with Make A Stand (1997) and Brave Inca (2006), McCoy still has two burning ambitions – to win the Martell Grand National at Aintree (the nearest he has come so far is two third-place finishes with Blowing Wind) and to ride 300 winners in a season.

An admirer of nine-times Derby-winning jockey Lester Piggott and former champion jump jockey John Francome, McCoy enjoys football (supporting Arsenal and visiting Highbury whenever possible) and golf. For the past few years he has hosted an annual charity golf day, inviting jockeys and other sporting celebrities to contribute.

McCririck

BORN IN APRIL 1940, JOHN McCririck is a larger-than-life, rather eccentric racing pundit for TV's Channel 4. Known for wearing a cape, outlandish deerstalker hat and waving his hands about, McCririck once voiced his right-wing views on BBC1's *Question Time*. He is vehemently opposed to jockeys using the whip and has, perhaps cruelly, been the subject of Paul Haigh's highly amusing column in *The Racing Post*.

RIGHT John McCririck in typically exurbriant mood

BELOW McCririck dons a red nose at Sandown Park in 2005

While some may question John's sanity, no one can doubt his status as the face of racing. Some love him, some loathe him – TV critic Nina Myskow famously said he had the charm of an armpit – but it is impossible to ignore his enthusiasm for the sport he loves.

John McCririck is tall, heavily built and smokes cigars. He has a voice as overbearing as his clothes and stalks the betting ring as if he owns it, but to his many admirers he's known as Big Mac. He worked as a bookmaker, sub-editor on Grandstand and as a writer on Sporting Life and for ITV between 1981 and 1984 before moving to the then newly-launched Channel 4. He has won two British press awards.

McCririck has added interest and enthusiasm to the sport over the years and isn't afraid to voice his opinions when he feels betting punters are being given a raw deal. His wife Jenny, also known as the Booby, plays an important part in all areas of his life, even driving him to race meets.

McManus

BORN IN 1951 IN LIMERICK, IRELAND, John Patrick McManus, better known as JP, has been a prominent figure in National Hunt racing over thirty years. In 1971 he became involved in racing as an on course bookmaker and in 1976 Cill Dara was his first horse to carry his now-famous green and gold hooped colours as an owner.

A fearless punter in his early days, he earned the nickname 'The Sundance Kid' and in 1982 won over £250,000 on Mister Donovan when he took the Sun Alliance Hurdle at Cheltenham. His tilts at the betting ring are legendary but he is now equally well known for the string of over a hundred racehorses in his ownership

JP's best horses to date have been the brilliant hurdler Istabraq, trained by Aiden O'Brien to win three consecutive Champion Hurdles, 1998-2000, and the Francois Doumen-trained Baracouda who won most of the long distance hurdle prizes from 2000-04.

Jonjo O'Neil became the recipient of most of McManus's horses when he was installed as trainer at JP's newly

ABOVE McManus at Aintree in 2005

acquired Jackdaw's Castle stables in the Cotswolds in 2001. The partnership has been a successful one, greatly enhanced by the arrival of AP McCoy as McManus's retained jockey.

With a fortune of over £255 million made from foreign currency trading, McManus finds time to play golf and in 2001, with John Magnier, took a major holding in Manchester United Football Club (no longer held). A shrewd businessman, he is well known for his generosity to charities.

Mill Reef

THE GREAT MILL REEF ARRIVED IN England in late 1969, having been shipped across the Atlantic by his owner and breeder, the American millionaire

BELOW Mill Reef in action in 1971, ridden by Geoff Lewis

Paul Mellon. Trained by Ian Balding, he made his mark as a two year-old, winning five out of six starts which set him up beautifully for the magical season to follow in 1971.

Having been beaten in the 2,000 Guineas by the magnificent Brigadier Gerard, he arrived at the Epsom Derby undaunted and duly won the race. The following month he took the prestigious Eclipse Stakes and the King George VI & Queen Elizabeth Diamond Stakes in the kind of form he took to Paris for the Prix de L'Arc de Triomphe, which was won in style.

After such a fantastic year Mill Reef might well have been retired, but he returned as a four year-old, winning at Longchamp and Epsom, although the fact he lacked a little zip was explained away as a virus problem.

After sustaining a broken leg in training, Mill Reef retired to the National Stud. There he had as much success as he did on the track, siring English Derby success Shirley Heights and Acamas, a French Derby winner.

National Hunt

NATIONAL HUNT IS THE OFFICIAL name for jump racing and has a much less glamorous reputation than flat racing. Broadly, jump races can be divided into steeplechases and hurdle races.

Steeplechases are run over distances from two to four and a half miles with horses jumping fixed fences which are at least four and a half feet high, while hurdle races, run over two to three and a half miles, involve smaller, less rigid obstacles which often collapse when hit by a jumping horse.

Horses are not allowed to race in a steeplechase until after 1 July in the year that they reach four years old, while horses are not permitted to run in a hurdle race until 1 July in the year that they turn three.

Both the Champion Hurdle and the Triumph Hurdle are held at Cheltenham over two miles and 200 yards. National Hunt races can also be roughly divided into five categories: bumpers, novice hurdles, hurdles, novice chases and chases.

BELOW Action at the 2005 National Hunt Festival at Cheltenham

ABOVE Champion National Hunt jockey Bryan Marshall takes three year old chestnut Sidown Hill over a jump

RIGHT Tikram, ridden by T Murphy, wins the Mildmay of Flete Handicap Chase at the 2004 Festival

Jump meetings are held year-round, although the season proper starts in mid-October with the Charlie Hall Chase being the first big race at Wetherby. Then a month later the first major meeting takes place when Cheltenham stages its Open meeting, featuring the Paddy Power Gold Cup.

Despite its less glamorous image and considerably less generous prize money for winners, attendance at jump-racing events is growing. There is also a current threat that more venues will be turned into all-weather tracks which will make the sport much cheaper to stage and less likely to be cancelled due to bad weather.

National Hunt flat races are also run over National Hunt courses but without any jumps; only horses aged four, five or six who have never raced in any other official race are eligible.

Newmarket

NEWMARKET HAS A LONG tradition of horseracing: it was the venue that saw Britain's first race run under written rules. It is also famous because King Charles II (1630-85) – who loved the town so much that he used to move his Court there – participated as a jockey in meetings and won a race on his own horse.

There are two courses in Newmarket: the Rowley Mile 'Course of Champions' used for spring and autumn racing and the July Course, host to the summer programme and known as the 'English Rose' of racing.

The former offers world-class facilities including the magnificent Millennium Grandstand, opened by the Queen in 2000, a far cry from the 17th Century when the King used to watch from the famous Bushes. If you fancy following in his footsteps, these are still there today, about a furlong and a half from the winning post.

As well as being home to Newmarket's

flagship event, the three-day July Festival, the July Course is also used as a music venue and has staged concerts by such luminaries as Katherine Jenkins, Jools Holland and Status Quo. The grand finale of the Festival features Europe's best sprint race, the Darley July Cup.

ABOVE Racing action at Newmarket

Nijinsky

NIJINSKY WAS BORN IN 1967 WITH an unusual scar on his coat, by Northern Dancer out of Flaming Page. Vincent O'Brien bought him from the Woodbine Sales on behalf of Charles Englehard, the diamond tycoon. Nijinsky, went on to become a superstar after bursting onto the scene in 1969 and was a hero of the flat.

He was extremely popular with the racing public (his popularity perhaps only surpassed by Arkle and Red Rum) which was well founded as his unprecedented achievements in 1970 in flat racing were like none seen before with his amazing turn of foot. Nijinsky inherited speed from his sire, Northern Dancer, as well as a fiery temper from dam Flaming Page, and proved a difficult horse to handle.

Vincent O'Brien's skills and experience as a trainer played an important role in shaping Nijinsky for racing. Despite his tendency to rear up and refuse to canter, he was handled with a great deal of patience and as a two year-old colt, made a promising start in the Erle Maiden Stakes, where he won eas-

ily. He furthered his victories with three wins at Ireland's biggest races including the Railway, Beresford – where he was given the run of his life by Deices – and Angeles Stakes. He also won the William Hill Dewhurst Stakes by four lengths and earned himself the title of Champion two year-old.

His three year-old debut in 1970 at the Gladness Stakes, Ireland, proved once again he was a winner when he left Deep Run and Prince Tenderfoot (the Coventry Stakes winner) behind

RIGHT Nijinsky in 1970

BELOW Lester Piggott on Nijinsky after winning the 1970 Epsom Derby

in the fastest time since Mahmoud in 1936.

The colt confirmed his form by winning the Irish Sweeps Derby easily by three lengths but he was to face older, more experienced horses in the King George VI & Queen Elizabeth Diamond Stakes. Despite facing winners including Karabas, Caliban, Hogarth and Crepellana, he drew effortlessly away from his rivals to win by two lengths.

Despite having a bout of ringworm which had seriously impacted on his training, Charles Englehard wished him to run in the St Leger to go with his victories in the 2,000 Guineas and the Derby to win the Triple Crown in 1970. He duly wrote his name in the history books and is the last horse to have achieved that feat.

Nijinsky, who won eleven of his thirteen starts, went on to sire stalwarts such as Lammtarra, Shahrastani and Shadeed. Lester Piggott believed he had never ridden a horse with as much natural ability as Nijinsky.

and rode to victory by four lengths. At odds of 7/4, he had become the shortest priced favourite for the Guineas since 1934.

In the Epsom Derby, many pundits were concerned about Nijinsky's staying power, because his sire hadn't been able to stay in the gruelling one and half miles in the Belmont Stakes; added to this, he faced fierce competition in Gyr and Stintino. After a tussle between French champion Gyre and Stintino, Nijinsky won by two and a half lengths

BELOW Nijinsky with Lester Piggott in 1970

Norton's Coin

WHEN IT COMES TO OUTSIDERS, Norton's Coin takes some beating. Born in 1981 to Grove Chance and sired by Mount Cassino, he only ran in the 1990 Cheltenham Gold Cup because an earlier entry deadline had been missed. Yet the chestnut gelding astounded racegoers and the watching world by romping home to victory in a time that eclipsed Dawn Run's course record.

The fact that the 100/1 outsider left favourite Desert Orchid trailing four lengths behind in third place made the feat even more remarkable. It was a true story of David and Goliath for owner/trainer Sirrell Griffiths and jockey Graham McCourt.

Norton's Coin won two other races at Cheltenham: the Caradon Mira Silver Trophy Chase in 1989 and 1991. In his only flat race, the 1991 Queen Alexandra Stakes at Royal Ascot, legendary jockey Lester Piggott could only coax him to eighth position out of the 13 starters.

The 1990 Gold Cup proved to be Norton's Coin's biggest ever race and he was retired in 1993 after an operation

TOP Norton's Coin led by owner/trainer, Sirrell Griffiths, at Cheltenham in 1991

RIGHT Norton's Coin in action in 1991

BELOW Racing at Cheltenham in 1990

failed to cure breathing problems. He died in 2001 of a suspected heart attack while grazing in his owner's field near Carmarthen in Wales.

Oaks

THE OAKS, HELD ANNUALLY AT Epsom during the Derby meeting, is a race over one-and-a-half miles for fillies that established itself in 1779 when the Earl of Derby declared his patronage and that it would be named after his Surrey home. He probably wore a beaming smile after that inaugural contest was won by his own horse, Bridget.

This is a much sought-after Classic that has been won over the years by such horses as Petite Etoile, Lupe and Ouija Board. The first Classic win for the all-conquering Godolphin stable came in the 1994 race when Balanchine, partnered by Frankie Dettori, romped to victory. Dettori may be still looking for his first Derby win but the Oaks has come his way three times.

Some races can be viewed as specialist events for certain jockeys and trainers, none more so in the case of Lester

ABOVE Exciting action at the 2005 Oaks

Piggott and Henry Cecil. Master jockey Piggott won the race no fewer than six times and trainer Cecil went one better between 1985 and 2000. This included four wins in five runnings, a record for any Classic race. Currently sponsored by Vodafone, the oaks was won in 2006 by Alexandrova.

O'Brien, Aiden

AFTER CUTTING SHORT HIS CAREER as a jockey at age 23, Aiden O'Brien saddled a double on his first day as a National Hunt trainer. On the retirement of Vincent O'Brien (no relation), Aiden was invited to take over the running of the Ballydoyle stable.

His first Classic success came in 1998 when King of Kings won 2,000 Guineas shortly after Istabraq had won the first of his three Champion Hurdles at Cheltenham. The chestnut colt Giant's Causeway, nicknamed the Iron Horse, won five Group One races for him in 2000, but fought like a tiger even in defeat and was never out of the first two in 13 starts. He went down by a neck to Tiznow in the Breeders' Cup, but was an unlucky loser.

In 2001 O'Brien sent out Galileo to win the Epsom Derby for Sue Magnier and Michael Tabor. This was followed by the Irish Derby and King George VI & Queen Elizabeth Diamond Stakes and helped the trainer break the record for most Group One races won in a season at 21.

2002 saw the 2,000 Guineas go to Rock of Gibraltar on his way to seven successive Group One races; Hawk Wing won the Eclipse after his defeat by stable companions Rock of Gibraltar and High Chaparral in the 2,000 Guineas and Derby respectively.

The next two years were comparatively quiet but, with incomparable powerhouse Kieron Fallon as his new stable jockey, Classic success came immediately with Footstepsinthesand winning the 2,000 Guineas and Virginia Waters taking the 1,000 Guineas. Oratorio took the Irish Champion Stakes and the Eclipse and everything seemed back to normal. O'Brien has already proved he has a touch of genius, but one feels the story has just begun.

O'Brien, Vincent

VINCENT O'BRIEN WAS BORN IN Churchtown, County Cork in 1917. Taking out a trainer's licence in 1943 and renting stables and a yard from his brother, he then began, from this modest start, to win most of jumping's major races in the late 1940s and early 1950s. He won the Cheltenham Gold Cup three times from 1948-50 with Cottage Rake before winning it again in 1953 with Knock Hard.

Hatton's Grace won him three consecutive Champion Hurdles from 1949 -51 in what was a remarkable training feat. Still O'Brien was running his horses on the flat with success and managed to win the Irish Cesarewitch with Cottage Rake. In 1950 he bought Ballydoyle and built it up to become one of Europe's most successful yards.

His association with the jumping game continued, winning the Grand National an unbelievable three years running with three different horses, Early Mist (1953), Royal Tan (1954) and Quare Times (1955).

Having achieved almost everything in National Hunt, O'Brien transferred his attention solely to the flat and took no time in winning the Prix de L'Arc de Triomphe with Ballymoss in 1958. His first Derby victory came in 1962 with Larkspur, followed by Sir Ivor (1968), Nijinsky (1970), Roberto (1972), The Minstrel (1977) and Golden Fleece (1982).

In the 1970s with Robert Sangster and John Magnier, O'Brien set up the Coolmore organisation which bought much of Northern Dancer's stock. They were highly successful and dominated racing with Lester Piggott and then Pat Eddery, adding their skill from the saddle. Alleged won two back to back Prix de L'Arcs and Detroit won for them in 1980.

Vincent O'Brien retired in the late 1980s, having been one of the greatest trainers the sport had seen and reaching the highest possible point in both codes. A legend and a genius.

Ormonde

THE UNDEFEATED ORMONDE came from excellent stock but did not impress his owner the Duke of Westminster as a foal. However, once he had matured, his trainer John Porter found he had a superior racing machine with a wonderful temperament.

In 1885 he raced only three times and only gave a hint of what he might be capable of. The following season opened with a win in the 2,000 Guineas. The English Derby contained a small field, due to the strong favouritism of Ormonde, and he didn't disappoint. His next big target was the Doncaster St Leger but two good wins leading up to this seemed to take nothing out of him and the final Classic of the season was won at a canter. This made Ormonde only

the fourth horse to complete the English Triple Crown.

Although finishing the previous year with a breathing problem, Ormonde continued to compete as a four year-old, still winning but finding it increasingly difficult. His last ever race was the Imperial Gold Cup at Newmarket in July 1887. He had competed in 15 races and never lost, leading his experienced trainer John Porter to comment that he was 'the greatest horse I've ever known.

RIGHT Fred Archer (1857-1886) on Ormonde, circa 1886 the year they won the Epsom Derby and the St Leger Stakes

O'Neill

BORN ON 13 APRIL 1952 IN County Cork, Jonjo O'Neill always aspired to be a jockey and served his apprenticeship with Michael Connolly at the Curragh. His first winner was on Lana, finishing in a dead heat in a local flat race on 9 September 1970. A move to England in 1973 proved the start of a long and successful career as both a jockey and then trainer despite suffering some horrendous injuries and battling cancer.

The 1977-78 season saw him ride a record-breaking 149 winners and become Champion Jockey, a title he held again in 1979-80. His career record of 901 winners included victories in the Champion Hurdle on Sea Pigeon (1980) and Dawn Run (1984). He has also won the Cheltenham Gold Cup twice on Alverton in 1979 and Dawn Run in 1986. Dawn Run entered the record books that day as the only horse to win both races. They have since been

immortalised in bronze overlooking the parade ring at Cheltenham.

O'Neill has been a successful trainer since he retired from the saddle and when Supreme Quest won the extended three-mile Novices' Handicap Hurdle at Uttoxeter in 2002, Jonjo achieved the distinction of becoming the first to win 100 races in a British season as both a jockey and a trainer.

ABOVE O'Neill with two of his horses, Rhinestone Cowboy (left) and Intersky Falcon, in 2003

Paget

ABOVE Paget leads in Golden Miller, ridden by Gerry Wilson, after he won the 1934 Grand National

RIGHT Dorothy Paget's Golden Miller in action

DOROTHY PAGET WAS ONE of racing's great eccentrics. Born in 1905, she inherited a fortune from her maternal grandfather. The daughter of Lord Queensborough, she owned horses under both codes but is best remembered for her success with Golden Miller, the winner of five consecutive Cheltenham Gold Cups between 1932 and 1936 and a Grand National in 1934.

She became the leading owner on the flat in 1943 when the Walter Nightingall-trained Straight Deal won her that year's Derby. Her blue and yellow colours were also carried successfully in pony races in the late 1930s.

Dorothy Paget was not an easy owner to deal with and her erratic sleeping patterns and demanding nature made life difficult for her trainers. Fulke Walwyn,

who trained Mont Tremblant to win the 1953 Cheltenham Gold Cup for her, was once famously talking to her on the phone for over eight hours. She would ring her trainers in the middle of the night to discuss her horses while her servants were kept up serving food.

Dorothy gambled heavily, was extremely superstitious and always wore the same coat to the races. Much of her inheritance was invested in bloodstock and many trainers were employed by her during her lifetime. She died in 1963.

Palio

STAGED ANNUALLY IN Siena, the Palio is Italy's foremost racing meet. It was first run on 16 August 1656 in honour of the holy apparition of 'Madonna de Provenzano', the Virgin Mary, who was seen near the old houses that belonged to Provenzano Salvani. Today, the race takes place every year on 2 July and 16 August and is held at the Piazza del Campo, where it remains one of the most popular events in the Italian calendar. In earlier times, many traditions and games took place alongside the main event; however, the Palio is the only tradition to have survived and preparations for this parade are slow and methodical.

Four days before the Palio, trials take place in the 'Campo' square which is specially turned into a race track. A thick layer of earth is spread on the ground and a row of mattresses placed against the walls at the dangerous corner of San Martino to protect any jockeys that may fall.

The square is ideal for the course as its shape is that of a mediaeval Roman amphitheatre closed at the base by the Palazzo Pubblico. Eleven streets run into it and there is room for 28,000 people to stand on the day of the event. There is a spectacular event with costumes and finery before the horses and riders appear. Jockeys have to take their horse around the track three times.

ABOVE Colour and excitement at the 2004 Palio race

Photo Finish

A PHOTO FINISH OCCURS IN A race when two or more horses cross the finishing line so close together that the naked eye cannot discern which came first.

This process used to involve a hand-cranked strip photograph being taken at the finish line but, with advances in tech-nology, today's preference is for digital photographs taken by specialised equipment. These can be triggered by means of a laser or may be photovoltaic (producing electricity directly from sunlight).

There are currently two ways of taking the photos. The most common is a camera that uses a single vertical slit instead of a shutter to produce a panoramic film strip. The other method involves a high-speed or movie camera that takes a continuous series of images.

With both methods, there are time markings on the bottom of the photo to help decide the horses' finishing order. As a horse travels at a speed of around five lengths per second, the timing is often in 1/5 seconds.

Stewards will announce whether the race is the subject of a photo finish and an objection can be triggered if other horses or jockeys interfered with the finishing order. When it is impossible to determine which horse has won, the race is declared a dead heat.

BELOW An image from a photo-finish camera used on the cover of Picture Post in 1948

Piggott

BORN ON 5 NOVEMBER 1935, Lester Piggott had the perfect pedigree to become a Champion Jockey. His father Keith was a successful jump jockey and mother Iris was from the famous Rickaby family.

Lester started race riding in 1948 and in that year rode his first winner at Haydock Park when just 12 years old. Champion apprentice at 15, he finished second in the 1952 Derby on Gay Time at the age of 16, his first Derby win following in 1954 on Never Say Die at 33/1. Showing his win-at-any-cost attitude, he soon fell foul of stewards who suspended him for six months after an incident at Royal Ascot. He spent the suspension away from his father's yard with Jack Jarvis at Newmarket, where his career was put back on track.

After the retirement of Gordon Richards, Piggott became stable jockey for Noel Murless at Newmarket in 1955. The highly successful partnership won the Derby twice with Crepello and St Paddy and, in 12 years together, harvested all the major races including seven Classics.

In 1966 Piggott opted to ride Valoris for Vincent O'Brien in the Oaks, leaving Murless searching for a rider for his filly Varinia, and the partnership ended later that year. 1968 saw his new association with brilliant Irish trainer O'Brien really take off. With Sir Ivor winning the Derby for American owner Raymond Guest, he then won another three English Derbys for O'Brien with Nijinsky in 1970, Roberto in 1972 and The Minstrel in 1977.

BELOW Piggott on Nijinsky winning the 2,000 Guineas in 1970

O'Brien, Piggott and owner Robert Sangster were a formidable force in all major races, and by winning the Derby on Empery in 1976 and Teenoso in 1983 Piggott completed his all-time record of nine Derby wins. 1981 brought a return to Noel Murless's old yard, Warren Place at Newmarket, when he became stable jockey to Henry Cecil. That year he became Champion Jockey and 1982 saw him take the title for the eleventh time. Five more English Classics were won before he announced his retirement in 1985. Racing would seem strange without 'the housewives' favourite'.

He started training from Newmarket with a stable of 74 horses producing 30 winners, the highlight being Cutting Blade's success at Royal Ascot. In 1987 he was given a three-year jail sentence for tax evasion. He served 366 days but, on his return, did not have sufficient horses to train so returned to race riding once more.

Encouraged by Vincent O'Brien, Piggott returned to the racetrack in the autumn of 1990. Just a few days later he landed one of the most valuable prizes of his career by winning the Breeders' Cup in America on Royal Academy at the age of 54. Then in 1992 he landed his thirtieth Classic by winning the 2,000 Guineas on Robert Sangster's Rodrigo Di Triano. A true genius.

Pipe

SON OF A WEST COUNTRY BOOK-maker, Martin Pipe was born in 1945. His first involvement in racing was riding as an amateur jockey and winning a point to point on Weather Permitting before he retired after breaking a thigh. Pipe turned his hand to training and had his first winner at Taunton when Hit Parade, ridden by Len Lungo, won a selling race in 1975.

His quest for winners gathered momentum from his Pond House Stables, Nicholshayne in Devon and he challenged the more orthodox ideas of training. Exercising his horses up steep hills, he introduced interval training and ran tests regularly on their blood while searching for any legitimate advantage to make his horses run faster.

His first big winner came in the Triumph Hurdle at Cheltenham when Baron Blakeney ridden by Paul Leech won in 1981. Pipe was still finding his stride, but by the end of the 1980s he began taking the major jump prizes with Strands of Gold winning the 1988 Hennessy Gold Cup and Bonanza Boy twice successful in the

ABOVE Pipe with Cyfor Malta in 2003

Welsh National (1988 and 1989).

His seasonal tally of winners was ever increasing, and after reaching the century in the 1986-87 season (106), he broke the 200 barrier with 208 in 1988-89. The horses were super-fit and, with Champion Jockey Peter Scudamore habitually making the running, the opposition was often run into the ground.

A Champion Hurdle came their way with Granville (1993). On the retirement of Peter Scudamore, Richard Dunwoody took over and won the

Grand National for Pipe with Minnehoma in 1994. Although the combination had their fair share of winners, it wasn't the happiest times for Pipe or the outstanding Dunwoody. David Bridgewater rode for a season before Tony McCoy took over the job in 1996 and won the Champion Hurdle with Make a Stand. From the 1995-96 season to the 2004-05 season Pipe was Champion Trainer and McCoy was, as ever, out on his own leading the Jockeys' Championship.

They dominated jump racing in this period and even when McCoy left to take up a very attractive offer from JP McManus, the Pipe bandwagon rolled on with the talented Timmy Murphy in the saddle. Pipe's principal owner was David Johnson, whose colours were regularly seen taking valuable prizes.

Martin Pipe's skill was evident on the flat; although having few runners, he managed to win the Cesarewitch twice, the Ascot Stakes at Royal Ascot four times and the Northumberland Plate twice, plus a Doncaster Cup (Group 3) and a two year-old Royal Ascot winner.

Pipe surprised the racing world by announcing his retirement in April 2006. Rarely has racing seen such a genius who, season after season, trained a mountain of winners. He changed other trainers' ideas and many had to follow to compete. He was meticulous in his search for winners which he invariably found.

RIGHT Martin Pipe using a bike to get around his stables

BELOW Pipe in 1993 at Chester

Pitman

JENNY PITMAN HAS BEEN DUBBED Aintree's first lady because she was the first woman trainer to win the Grand National – to date, no other female trainer has achieved this. The horse in question, Corbiere, won the coveted title in 1983. She then went on to repeat the feat 12 years later with 40/1 shot Royal Athlete. Jenny was the second woman to be granted a professional licence to train horses and has since gone on to register 800 winners.

Jenny Pitman comes from a racing family; indeed, her son Mark is a jockey who was beaten into second place on her Garrison Savannah at the Grand National, but who also won a Gold Cup on another of her charges. He became her assistant trainer on retiring from riding and was later a trainer in his own right.

Jenny's then-husband, Richard, also came second on Crisp in the Grand National in 1973 and, since retiring from the sport has become a racing commentator for television. Other titles she has won include the Cheltenham Gold Cup which she won twice with Burrough Hill Lad and Garrison Savannah. Jenny Pitman was awarded the OBE for services to racing in 1998 and has penned a best-selling autobiography.

ABOVE Jenny Pitman at Cheltenham in 1998

Point to Point

THE WORD STEEPLECHASING actually derives from point-to-point racing as the hunting types who originally raced over natural terrain often designated that the race took place between one steeple and the next. Steeplechasing itself became a separate entity in the 19th Century when professional elements took over, leaving 'point to point' an amateur haven.

All such events were run separately and it took until 1913 before the Master of Hounds Point-to-Point Association drew up an established set of rules. At the time ladies and gentlemen competed against each other but, from 1929 to 1967, the ladies were limited to their own races.

In 1935 point to point racing came under the umbrella of the National Hunt Committee, whose rulings from that time constitute the basis for racing today. Professional riders were definitely banned, courses had to be approved by the Inspector of Courses and any horse that had spent time in a licensed trainer's yard was ineligible.

Lady riders can now ride against their

male counterparts in keeping with modern times and sixteen is the age at which they can take part. Although under the auspices of the National Hunt authorities, point-point still retains elements of a bygone age.

Prix De L'Arc

INTRODUCED WITH THE IDEA OF creating a race that would be an end-of-season test of the top International horses, the Prix de L'Arc de Triomphe was first run in 1920. It has since become one of the world's most prestigious races and, run over 1½ miles on the first Sunday in October at Longchamp in the Bois de Boulogne, Paris, it is the highlight of the French calendar.

The first winner of the race, the three year-old Comrad, was trained in Newmarket, England by Peter Gilpin. His success was emulated by James Crawford with Parth three years later, but from then on the race was dominated by the French until the late 1950s and 1960s.

The race gained an international flavour with the unbeaten Ribot winning from his Italian base two years running in 1955-56 and fellow countryman Molvedo in 1961, while the Irish had success with Ballymoss (1958) and Levmoss (1969).

There have been some outstanding individual performances over the years with Sea Bird's victory in 1965 and

Dancing Brave's scintillating triumph in 1986. Star Appeal won the race for Germany in 1975 at the longest odds ever of 119/1.

Females have done well in this race, and the years from 1979-83 saw five consecutive fillies take the prize in the shape of Three Troikas, Detroit, Gold River, Akiyda and All Along. Prior to this, Alleged, trained by Vincent O'Brien, had won two years running, emulating Tantieme's efforts of 1950-51.

Recent victors such as Montjeu (1999) Sinndar (2000) and Hurricane Run (2005) have been impressive winners in Europe's most competitive all-age race.

Queen & Queen Mother

ABOVE The Queen enters into the spirit of Ascot with an impressive hat in 2004

TOP The Queen and Queen Mother at the 1985 Derby. The Queen Mother appears to be enjoying the race more!

THE ROYAL FAMILY HAVE BEEN heavily involved in horseracing over the years with Charles II linked closely to Newmarket in the 17th Century and Queen Anne being instrumental in the birth of racing at Ascot.

George IV, when still the Prince of Wales, won the Derby with Sir Thomas in 1788 and nearly a hundred years later the then Prince of Wales, later Edward VII, established stud farms at Sandringham and won the Derby three times with Persimmon (1896), Diamond Jubilee (1900) and Minoru (1909).

Our current Queen's father, George VI, won the fillies' Triple Crown with Sun Chariot in 1942 and the Derby with Big Game in the same year. His last

Classic winner was Hypericum, winner of the 1,000 Guineas in 1946 – a horse whose trainer, Cecil Boyd-Rochfort, duly became the Queen's trainer on the death of her father.

The Queen is a very knowledgeable and hugely enthusiastic owner. Aureole finished second to Pinza in the Derby in her coronation year of 1953 before winning the King George VI & Queen Elizabeth Stakes a year later. Pall Mall took the 2,000 Guineas in 1958, once more trained by Boyd-Rochfort, a year after Lester Piggott had ridden the Noel Murless-trained Carrozza to victory in the Oaks.

The 1960s were relatively lean times for Her Majesty but, with Lord

of useful animals in training with Sir Michael Stoute, Andrew Balding and Richard Hannon among others, the outlook is hopeful.

The Queen Mother raced her horses under National Hunt rules with great success. 1949 saw her join the ranks of jump racing and soon, with the help of Royal trainer Peter Cazalet, won the King George VI Chase with Monicou in 1950. Cazalet trained 250 winners for her and tasted drama in the 1956 Grand National when Devon Loch, ridden by Dick Francis, suddenly collapsed on the run-in

LEFT The Queen Mother inspects a racehorse at Sandown in 1971

BELOW The Queen Mother with her horse Bella Macrae in 2001

Porchester as her racing manager, the Royal Stud was reorganised and Classic winners were forthcoming with Highclere (1,000 Guineas and French Oaks, 1974) and Dunfermline (Oaks and St Leger, 1977). Both horses were trained by Dick Hern at West Ilsley .

The Queen enjoys nothing more than winning at Royal Ascot and her horses have been successful there over the years. The Derby is still the only Classic she hasn't won but, with a large number

when in a clear lead. It is unlikely anyone will find the answer to that mystery.

Fulke Walwyn trained for the Queen Mother on Peter Cazalet's death in 1975 and carried on the good work with such horses as Game Spirit (which won 21 races), The Argonaut and Special Cargo, winner of the Whitbread Gold Cup in a thrilling finish in 1984. The Queen Mother was one of the jumping game's most enthusiastic and devoted owners with over 400 winners to her name.

Quixall Crossett

IT IS NOT OFTEN THAT A RACE-horse gains celebrity status for being a failure but that is exactly what happened to steeplechaser Quixall Crossett.

With a name derived from former 1960s Manchester United player Albert Quixall and High Crossett Farm where he was born, the 16 year-old gelding had been racing since he was five and had built up a cult following thanks to his losing streak.

TOP Quixall Crossett at Southwell in 2001

RIGHT Quixall Crossett in his usual place at the back of the field

BELOW Ridden by Gary Lyons at Haydock Park in 1999

A 66/1 outsider in his 100th race at Southwell in July 2001, Quixall Crossett pulled up halfway through the three-mile race but had been judged the best turned-out horse in the parade ring beforehand. One female admirer was even wearing a scarf matching the mauve/blue/white colours of his jockey's silks.

There were public calls for his trainer, farmer Ted Caine, to retire him following his 103rd outing at Ayr on 18 November 2001 when he trailed the first horse home by more than 100 lengths.

It was not all doom and gloom for Quixall Crossett, however, as although he never managed to make it first past

the winning post, he did register two second placings and six thirds in his 103 races, netting career earnings of more than £8,000.

Racecourses

NO TWO RACECOURSES ARE ALIKE and, with investment taking place at so many courses, the range and quality of facilities is improving by the year. Ascot and Kempton Park have both received major facelifts and it's difficult to find a course that hasn't either had or is not contemplating some kind of refurbishment, for these are boom times for racing.

All courses have their idiosyncrasies. For instance, Epsom has a left hand turn coming into the straight, as have Aintree and Cheltenham, but Ascot turns to the right. This is an important factor for trainers with horses who perform well if the track turns in a certain direction. Similarly, undulating terrain can find some animals out. The Tattenham Corner turn at Epsom, which takes the racers down into a dip before a climb to the finish, has done for a number of quality horses.

Aintree's enormous fences take their toll – and if the obstacles aren't enough, that endless run-in to the line from the last fence will favour more dogged performers. Jockeys will often make the difference on those occasions. Newmarket, the home of English racing, has vast open spaces which accommodates two separate courses and is home to the 1,000 and 2,000 Guineas. Somehow a mile at Newmarket looks much longer than anywhere else.

Many smaller tracks have a charm of their own. Windsor, for instance, has a beautiful setting and a figure of eight course, as has Fontwell which features National Hunt racing. The latter was voted 'the best little racecourse in the south east' in a survey of racegoers. Chester is another smaller track whose Chester Cup week meeting in May attracts great attention.

ABOVE Newmarket is a vast racecourse

BELOW Windsor racecourse is delightfully pretty

Red Rum

RED RUM WAS BORN IN 1965 AT Rossenarra Stud, County Kilkenny, Ireland. In less than two years he had won his first race at Aintree, dead-heating in the Thursby Plate over five furlongs.

At the time it would have seemed unbelievable that this horse bred for flat-racing could return years later to win a record three Grand Nationals. He won three races on the flat before racing over hurdles and fences, and passed through many owners' and trainers' hands before joining the yard of trainer Donald 'Ginger' McCain. He persuaded owner Noel La Mare, who shared his dream to win the National, to buy the horse which, when it arrived, was lame and suffering from pedalostitis. McCain trained his horses on Southport beach so luckily, with the aid of the salt water and sand, Rummy had landed on his feet.

Up to his first Grand National in 1973 he had won five races or been second in all of his eight starts. When the tapes went up for the National, Red Rum ridden by Brian Fletcher, was 9/1 co-favourite with top weight Crisp. Trained by Fred Winter and ridden by Richard Pitman, Crisp was

RIGHT Red Rum wins the Grand National for the third time with jockey Tommy Stack in 1977

BELOW Red Rum's grave next to the winning post at Aintree

a classy Australian-bred chaser who had what looked an unassailable lead as he jumped the last fence. However, Red Rum came from out of the pack to chase Crisp home and, receiving a stone and nine pounds from him, nailed his rival on the line to win by three quarters of a length. Both had jumped brilliantly and Crisp was a gallant loser.

In 1974 Red Rum now carried top weight in the National of 12 stone two pounds after another successful season

ABOVE Red Rum exercises on Southport beach in 1985

of four wins and three seconds. A small, compact horse, he was an agile, clever jumper and showed all these qualities once again to win his second successive National. In doing so, ridden again by Brian Fletcher, he beat the former Cheltenham Gold Cup winner L'Escargot. In 1975 he finished second to L'Escargot on the heavy ground he hated, and, again in 1976, he finished second to Rag Trade.

Then, with Tommy Stack in the saddle and carrying 11 stone eight pounds, he beat Churchtown Boy by 25 lengths to record his record-breaking third National win.

One of the most popular chasers of all time, he retired in 1979 after missing the 1978 race through injury. Life as a celebrity then took over, opening shops, supermarkets and working for charity. He was humanely put down in 1995, aged 30, and was buried next to the Aintree winning post.

Richards

BORN IN 1904 INTO A FAMILY OF 12 children, Gordon Richards, the son of a Shropshire miner, dominated the Jockeys' Championship from 1925-53. In this period he won the title 26 times with only three jockeys in as many years wresting it from him.

Richards rode his first winner on Gay Lord at Leicester in 1921 and won his first Jockeys' Championship just four years later. However, the 1926 season was only to yield five winners as he spent most of this year on the sidelines suffering from tuberculosis. Recovering well, he took off where he started and, riding for Martin Hartigan, regained his title the following year.

In 1932 he became stable jockey to the powerful yard of Fred Darling at Beckhampton and in 1933 rode 12 consecutive winners over three days. He broke Fred Archer's record of winners in a season that year by riding 259 and, in his time with Darling and, later, Noel Murless, rode such horses as Sun Chariot, Big Game, Owen Tudor, Tudor Minstrel and Queenpot to Classic victories. Renowned for his quickness at the

RIGHT Gordon Richards on the Queen's horse, Gay Time, after winning the Gordon Stakes at Goodwood in 1952

BELOW Richards on Blue Train in 1947

starting gate, Richards was also skilled in keeping a true line.

Despite all this, winning the Derby had eluded him. Then at his twenty-eighth attempt he won it in 1953 on Sir Victor Sassoon's Pinza, beating the Queen's Aureole by four lengths.

Now Sir Gordon, Richards retired in 1954 having won a record 26 Championships, 13 Classics and a total of 4,870 winners. He became a successful trainer for owners Sir Michael Sobell and Lady Beaverbrook from his bases at Beckhampton, Ogbourne Baisey and Whitsbury, and trained among others the champion miler Reform in 1967.

After retiring from training in 1970, Gordon Richards became racing manager for Lady Beaverbrook and the Sobells. He died in 1986.

LEFT Richards relaxing at the stables in 1947

Rous

HENRY JOHN ROUS WAS born in 1795, the second son of the Earl of Stradbroke, and entered the Royal Navy as a midshipman in 1808. In the earliest part of his career, he was no stranger to action and a medal for bravery was his reward. By 1823 he had made captain and for the next six years India and New Holland were his home.

In 1834 as commander of the Pique, he achieved a degree of fame as he nursed his damaged ship across the three thousand mile Atlantic after it had ran ashore in Labrador.

On retiring from the Navy Rous, always a keen sportsman, took up the post of steward at the Jockey Club in 1838, which he held down until his death in 1877. In 1855, the post of public handicapper came his way and he took to this role with relish, producing the still valid weight-for-age scale.

Rous seemed to have boundless energy and, although he acquired a rep-utation as a dictator, laid down many of the rules for the Jockey Club today. His book *The Laws And Practice Of Horseracing* became the bible for the sport. He also took a hands-on stance at Newmarket where he managed the Duke of Bedford's stables for a consid-erable time.

Scudamore

BY THE TIME PETER SCUDAMORE retired in 1993, he had set a new record of 1,678 career wins with 221 coming in the 1988-89 season to cement his place in history as the most successful National Hunt jockey of all time. These achievements have since been eclipsed by Richard Dunwoody and Tony McCoy.

Scudamore had racing in his blood as father Michael had won the 1959 Grand National on Oxo. 'Scu' – as he was affectionately known – was given his break by trainer David Nicholson, who employed him in his yard, and he first tasted victory on Rolyat at Devon and Exeter in 1979. But it was as stable jockey to Martin Pipe that he enjoyed greatest success.

Although he never managed to win the Grand National, third on Corbière in 1985 being his best placing, Scu did claim the Champion Hurdle twice (in 1988 and 1993). His 1988-89 record-breaking season obliterated the previous record of 149 wins set by Jonjo O'Neill.

A keen cricketer throughout his life, he was Champion Jockey a record eight times, enjoying a run of consecutive titles from 1985-92.

Following his retirement, Scudamore has become a top TV horseracing commentator and writes for the *Daily Mail*.

ABOVE Peter Scudamore training on the Gallops at Lambourne

BELOW Scudamore jumping a fence at Fontwell in 1992

See You Then

SIRED BY 1967 DERBY WINNER Royal Palace and out of a flat-bred mare, See You Then found his future in National Hunt Racing.

Trained for most of his career by Nicky Henderson at Lambourn, his racecourse appearances were limited on account of his fragile legs and so was referred to by the press on numerous occasions as See You When. In 1984 he won a couple of decent hurdles and finished second in the Triumph Hurdle at Cheltenham.

John Francome was to ride him in his first attempt at Champion Hurdle glory in 1985, only to be injured on the day. Steve Smith-Eccles stepped in for the ride and won at odds of 16/1. The strongly fancied Browne's Gazette, ridden by Dermot Browne, veered violently across the track at the start, putting paid to his chances.

After wining the Oteley Hurdle in 1986 on one of his rare appearances that season, See You Then went on to successfully defend his crown in the Champion Hurdle. The following season he was rarely on a racecourse but,

skilfully handled by his trainer and now regular pilot Steve Smith-Eccles, he went on to make it a hat-trick of championships.

A quick and accurate jumper, See You Then deserves his place amongst the top hurdlers.

RIGHT On his way to landing the 1987 Champion Hurdle at Cheltenham

BELOW See You Then after winning the race

Starting Stalls

WHEN FIRST SEEN IN BRITAIN IN 1965, starting stalls were regarded as a bit of a novelty only seen in a number of imported films from the United States. Subsequently, they appeared at all flat race meetings and eliminated all the ugly jockeying we had come to accept at the start of races. Provided the horse emerges instantly from his individual stall once the front gate has been released he stands an equal chance of victory.

The stalls come in blocks of ten individual units and are distributed around the country from a depot based at Newmarket, which has the capacity to cover seven meetings a day. The blocks can be moved around the course as needed and come with a team of at least eight handlers who have the responsibility of installing the horses in an efficient and safe manner. The theory is simple but the practice can often be fraught, as individual equines do not always play ball.

Some horses will enter the stalls with the minimum of fuss, others will comply after a gentle coaxing but there are those who simply don't enjoy the expe-

rience and need expert cajoling. It is not unknown for some runners to flatly refuse to be enclosed and be withdrawn from a race.

ABOVE A dramatic start to a race in Singapore

Steeplechasing

THE ROOTS OF STEEPLECHASING originated in Ireland in the late 17th Century, when 'pounding matches' took place over chosen country. The idea was to pound your opponent into the ground by outlasting them on typically heavy horses that could cope with the rough ground and could jump.

BELOW The first steeplechases ran through the countryside – from church steeple to church steeple

By the mid 18th Century, chosen courses with a winning post of a predetermined landmark (often a church steeple) were established. Although commonly known as a steeplechase, the original term used was steeplehunt. It has been cited that a 1752 match over four and a half miles from Buttevant Church in County Cork to the spire of St Leger Church between Edmund Blake and a Mr O'Callaghan was one of the first recognisable races to take place and contained the draft conditions for the Irish steeplechase held in 1803. A sweepstake of claret, port and rum put the steeplechase firmly on the Irish calendar in 1807 which described a six-mile 'cross-country match race'.

As the industrial revolution began to consume forests in England, stag hunting was replaced with fox hunting. The slower horses that were unable to jump were inadequate for the quick prey that would race across open country. Unsurprisingly, faster horses that could jump became the mounts of choice.

Thoroughbred sires were increasingly crossed on grade mares of various types to breed faster animals. Generally in Ireland thoroughbreds were considered essential in breeding hunters and chasers and a number of half-bred mare families were established, which have provided steeplechasing with some of its greatest winners.

One of the earliest recorded races in England took place in the 1790s between Loraine Hardy and the Hon. Mr Willoughby's horses for 1,000 guineas over nine miles from Melton Mowbray to Dalby Wood. Later flags were introduced so that riders could follow an agreed course to the finishing post and in 1813 in County Roscommon, Ireland, the six-mile course included six walls over five feet in height and several wide ditches.

The first known steeplechase course was constructed in Bedford in 1810. It consisted of eight fences at four foot six inches high and horses entered into races here had to be certified hunters. The St Albans steeplechase, established in 1830, was to influence many other courses around the country.

The first flat race held at Aintree took place in 1829 and the course included 20 fences in two circuits. It was significant because the course was enclosed and fences flagged along the route. Cheltenham's first steeplechase came later in 1841.

Until established courses were laid out,

it was not uncommon for supporters of one horse and rider to try and sabotage the route for opponents. Finally, with many critics of steeplechasing, the Grand National Hunt Committee was formed to control the sport and assess penalties. Steeplechasing was recognised by the Jockey Club in 1866 and in Ireland the Irish National Hunt Steeplechase Committee was established in 1869. The Grand National Hunt Committee changed its name to National Hunt Committee in 1889, the name by which it is still known today.

ABOVE Modern steeplechases take place on specially prepared tracks, such as Aintree

Stoute

BORN IN 1945, MICHAEL Stoute has been a major force in the training ranks for over 30 years. A great follower of cricket, he left his native Barbados in 1965 to pursue a career in racing.

After assisting such trainers as Pat Rohan in the North, Stoute set up in Newmarket in 1972. Two years later, he had won his first Classic when Fair Salinia ridden by Greville Starkey, won the Oaks. He had made an immediate impact and in 1981 he became Champion Trainer and won his first Derby with the Aga Khan's Shergar. An Irish Derby and King George VI & Queen Elizabeth Diamond Stakes followed his record ten-length Epsom victory. Stoute has won the Derby a further three times with Shahrastani (1986), Kris Kin (2003) and North Light (2004).

A steady flow of top-class horses like Russian Rhythm, King's Best, Golan, and Entrepreneur has emerged from his Freemason Lodge Stables in Newmarket to capture international prizes. His tal-

ent has been to improve older horses at four and five, as with Singspiel who won the 1996 Japan Cup, and 1997 Dubai Cup. Pilsudski followed this example by winning the Japan Cup in 1997 after winning the 1996 Breeders' Cup and the 1997 Eclipse, Irish Champion Stakes and the Champion Stakes.

Not content with winning most of the major flat races, Stoute took the 1990 Champion Hurdle with Kribensis. A master of his trade, he was knighted in 1998 and the seven times Champion Trainer remains at the top of his game.

RIGHT A cheerful Sir Michael Stoute at the Breeders' Cup in New York, 2005

BELOW The Queen at the 2003 Derby watching her horse, Chief Yeoman, which Stoute (right) trained

Studs & Breeding

EVERYBODY UNDERSTANDS the function of a stud farm, which is essentially to breed horses. But in the case of thoroughbreds, this becomes a slightly more sophisticated operation which, even in the most expert of hands, doesn't necessarily produce the animal of expectation. Having said this, if two horses with proven pedigrees are brought together for mating purposes, the breeder is always in with a sporting chance of producing something a little bit special.

Whilst not the only stud in the UK, the National Stud is the most famous establishment, situated a couple of miles away from racing's headquarters at Newmarket. Within its five hundred acres of land it can offer a wide range of services, such as boarding, quarantine, preparation for sale plus training and educational facilities. At any one time it can accommodate eight stallions and two hundred mares spread over an area containing nine yards.

The National Stud dates back to 1916 but did not move to its present sight until the 1960s when it became what is known as a stallion station. The operation is proud of its record, having produced an English Derby winner in Never Say Die and acquiring the services of the great Mill Reef. The Stud is happy to open its doors to interested parties and runs guided tours during the spring and summer. The National Stud is not the only farm in Newmarket, which can also boast Cheveley Park, Sheikh Mohammed's Darley, and Lanwades Stud.

In Ireland the Coolmore Stud, headed by John Magnier, proclaimed itself 'the pre-eminent stallion station in the world' in 2006 – a statement it was hard to argue with as Sadler's

ABOVE A stud groom steadies a horse before its visit to the sales ring at Doncaster

Wells, Rock of Gibraltar and Galileo were amongst its roster. Its stallions have sired over one hundred group winners every year since 1996. The Coolmore group also has farms in the United States and Australia.

The Juddmonte Farms group is yet another international set-up that has made its presence felt, having six farms in the UK and Ireland and three in the US. Juddmonte can claim to have bred around one hundred and 20 group winners, which include 13 Classic races.

The Godolphin Stables have their own stud facilities in Dubai but the late Sheik Maktoum, a founder member, owned the Gainsborough Stud until his death in 2006. Gainsborough's operations take place in England, Ireland and the United States.

Swinburn

WALTER SWINBURN, BORN on 7 August 1961, enjoyed a hugely successful career as a flat-racing jockey during the 1980s and 1990s. His father Wally had been a flat jockey in Ireland and the young Walter was apprenticed to Frenchie Nicholson and Reg Hollinshead, following in the footsteps of the likes of Pat Eddery.

Nicknamed 'the Choirboy', Swinburn's first victory came on Paddy's Luck at Kempton Park in July 1978, but it was riding Shergar to victory in the 1981 Epsom Derby that brought him fame and fortune. The pair were placed third after descending Tattenham Hill, but they showed the other competitors a clean set of shoes in the straight and, despite easing up as they approached the line, eventually finished a massive ten lengths in front of their nearest challenger to register the widest winning margin in the history of the race.

Shergar had been trained by the Barbados-born Sir Michael Stoute with whom Swinburn struck up a successful relationship that resulted in eight British Classics and a Prix de L'Arc de Triomphe title.

In 1983, Swinburn won the Arc de Triomphe on All Along and three years later rode Shahrastani to his second Derby crown. The following year saw Unite give him the Oaks title and he claimed two more Classics before the end of the decade (the 2,000 Guineas on Doyoun in 1988 and the 1,000 Guineas on Musical Bliss the following year).

He reclaimed the 1,000 Guineas in 1992 on Hatoof and retained his title a year later on Sayyedati before riding his

ABOVE Swinburn in action on Sharastani at Epsom in 1986

RIGHT A jubilant Swinburn on Lammtarra after winning the 1995 Epsom Derby

third Epsom Derby winner, Lammtarra, in 1995. He fell badly on Liffey River in Kong Kong in February 1996, however, and missed the next eight months' racing.

Swinburn's success on the track had brought other problems as he struggled to keep his weight down and he found himself plummeting deeper into the misery of bulimia and alcoholism; a public admission of his plight followed in March 1997.

Swinburn's weight problems continued and he did not participate during the 1999 season, but returned at Wolverhampton's all-weather course in

March 2000. Even though Diamond Flame finished next to last in the Don Allen Retirement Handicap, he enjoyed getting back into the saddle but finally retired the following month. At the beginning of 2005, Swinburn took over the running of Church Farm stables in Hertfordshire where he had been his father-in-law Peter Harris' assistant.

Syndicate

RACEHORSE SYNDICATES ALLOW members of the public who do not have unlimited funds to buy a share of their own thoroughbred. It means that you do not have to be a millionaire to experience the ups and downs of horseracing ownership.

Syndicates have become more numerous as horseracing's appeal has grown and the advent of the internet has meant that the opportunity to enjoy a day at the races with all the privileges and excitement of an owner is much more readily available.

Being a syndicate member usually entitles the person to go to race days, visit the stables and see their own horse in training, as well as joining in the social side of racehorse ownership.

Each member receives an official owner's badge each time their horse runs, unless there are so many shares in the horse that these are restricted and participation is on a rotation basis. These permit access to all areas that are accessible to owners and trainers, such as the owner's viewing area in the grandstand; the owner's/trainer's bar and restaurant; the parade ring to meet the jockey before the race and, most importantly, the winner's enclosure if the horse wins or is placed.

ABOVE A good racehorse is expensive. This yearling was sold for 500,000 euros in 2005

Taaffe

PAT TAAFFE, HAILED BY MANY AS Ireland's greatest National Hunt jockey of all time, was born with horseracing in his blood on 12 March 1930 in Rathcoole, County Dublin. Three years prior to winning his first Grand National on Quare Times in 1955, his father Tom had trained Mr What to the same title.

It was in the 1960s, however, that Pat hit the headlines, winning three consecutive Cheltenham Gold Cups on the legendary Arkle between 1964 and 1966. He also won the prestigious race two years later, this time on Fort Leney, before going on to register

his second Grand National in 1970 on Gay Trip.

While Richard Dunwoody is hailed as the most successful rider of the Cheltenham Festival in the modern age with 18 winners, Pat Taaffe is the most successful of all with 25 wins. He is also the most successful jockey in the Queen Mother Champion Chase event with five victories: Fortria in 1960 and 1961, Ben Stack in 1964, Flyingbolt in 1966 and Straight Fort in 1970.

Becoming a trainer once he retired from the saddle, Taaffe won chasing's Blue Riband with Captain Christy in 1974. He received a heart transplant in March 1991 but died before seeing his trainer son Tom again engrave the family surname on the Gold Cup with Kicking King in 2005.

Tattersalls

WHEN FOUNDED IN 1766 BY SIR Richard Tattersall, Tattersalls became the first bloodstock auction house in the world. Today its function remains the same and is regarded as Europe's leader in the field. Sixteen times a year a total of 10,000 horses are on offer at either Newmarket or Fairyhouse in Ireland.

This international organisation has built a reputation for offering the finest thoroughbreds in the world and potential buyers from all over the globe gravitate to the sales.

Seven sales a year are held at Newmarket, the October Yearling Sale being regarded as the one from which potential Classic winners are going to emerge. The Autumn Horses In Training Sale is claimed to be the largest of its kind anywhere in the world and the December Sale, which offers both brood-mares and foals, is also a leading event.

Tattersalls should not, however, be regarded simply as a money-making machine. In 2005, the company sponsored a number of races both on the flat and over jumps, taking in meetings in

ABOVE Tattersalls' modern new premises

Moscow, Penang and Serbia, not to mention the Dubai World Cup. Its October Auction Stakes, Europe's major sales race, is held at Newmarket and is worth £250,000.

Tetrarch

THE TETRARCH WAS BOUGHT FOR 1,300 guineas by trainer Atty Persse at Doncaster Sales in September 1912. A grey colt by Roi Herode, he had large white blotches all over his hind-quarters. Persse intended to retain a half-share but his cousin, Captain Dermot McCalmont, decided he wanted to own him outright.

In April of 1913 Persse organised a trial against older horses, so convincing was the Tetrarch that Persse was ready for a large gamble. The Tetrarch made his debut in the Maiden Two Year Old Plate at Newmarket, and so well had the stable kept secret his ability, he was allowed to start at 5/1. He won at a canter by four lengths. The Derby meeting was his next stop, where he made the Woodcote Stakes a procession and followed that by winning the Coventry Stakes at Royal Ascot by ten lengths. Crowds poured in to see the Tetrarch wherever he ran, and he won his next race at Sandown at odds of 100/12 on.

Described by his regular jockey, the brilliant Steve Donoghue, as the fastest horse he had ever sat on, he won three further races that year at Goodwood, Derby and Doncaster with ease. He injured himself at the beginning of his three year-old season and was retired to stud where he sired 80 winners, three of which won the St Leger and one, Tetratema, won the 1920 2,000 Guineas – not a bad record for a horse sometimes referred to as the 'Rocking Horse' or the 'Spotted Wonder'.

BELOW Tetrarch was famous for the white patches over his body

Unexplained

OCCASIONALLY RACING THROWS up inexplicable events; here we look at two wildly contrasting occurrences that continue to baffle the experts.

Whatever Devon Loch may have achieved in his racing life he will only ever be remembered for a failure beyond comprehension which was captured on celluloid and is regularly aired whenever major Grand National incidents are pinpointed.

HM Queen Elizabeth the Queen Mother's horse Devon Loch seemed to be on his way to a famous victory in the 1956 race, when, with the winning post less than fifty metres away, he inexplicably took a half-jump where no obstacle existed. As jockey Dick Francis tried desperately to get him back on his feet and running again, ESB came past to win the race. Devon Loch failed to finish, leaving his owner disappointed but philosophical. The public remained completely stunned.

Many theories were voiced at the time and still are to the present day, the favourite being that the horse took the shadow from the adjacent water jump as being another fence. Cramp in his hind legs became another favourite but the suggestion of a heart attack didn't hold up, for shortly after the race he showed no signs of distress. It is mystery that will never be resolved and a story that jockey Francis, who went on to write whodunits, could never have created.

Shergar was a very special horse but he will be forever remembered for his unresolved disappearance.

Winning six races out of eight, including the 1981 Derby by a record distance, the horse had been retired to the Aga Khan's Ballymany Stud in

ABOVE Shergar in his Newmarket stables in 1980

County Kildare with great things expected of him. But on 8 February 1983 on a murky night, just as the breeding season approached, Shergar was snatched at gunpoint.

A ransom demand for £1.5m, received by an Irish radio station, turned out to be a hoax and, despite the owners' willingness to talk to the kidnappers, the trail eventually went cold.

As on all such occasions, various theories were put forward as to Shergar's whereabouts, including one that suggested the horse had been spirited away to the Middle East for breeding purposes.

The IRA were in the frame from the start but have never laid claim to the kidnapping. One ex-Provisional did come forward with a fairly plausible story which suggested that the IRA did indeed snatch the horse but were unable to control the highly-strung beast. Consequently they had to kill him and bury his remains. Not the ignominious end anybody would have wished upon a great horse, if indeed it is true.

Vintage Crop

A CONTENDER FOR IRELAND'S most famous horse, Vintage Crop took the racing world by storm in 1993 when he became the first foreign-trained horse to win Australia's richest prize.

It was the first year that European horses had been invited to participate in the Melbourne Cup and Irish trainer Dermot Weld, an ex-rugby player and a vet, had experience of racing Down Under following a spell early in his career with local trainer Tommy Smith. Weld was also the first to take a horse to win an American Triple Crown race, so had experience of international competition.

Vintage Crop won the Irish St Leger the same year and retained the title again in 1994. He travelled to Australia to defend his Melbourne Cup title but ran home seventh.

Vintage Crop retired to the Irish National Stud in County Kildare after finishing third in the 1995 Melbourne Cup, with career prize money of more than $2,375,000. He is visited by thousands of well-wishers every year and is a popular attraction, often invited to christen a new grandstand or attend a special race meeting. He has also been immortalised with a statue at the Curragh racecourse.

ABOVE Vintage Crop (right) running in the Royal Cup at Ascot in 1994

BELOW MJ Kinane riding Vintage Crop to victory at the 1993 Irish St Leger

Walsh

RIGHT Ruby celebrates after winning the 2005 Grand National, on Hedgehunter

OPPOSITE Walsh riding Asian Maze to victory in the Scottish and Newcastle Hurdle at Aintree in 2006

BELOW Ted Walsh at the Cheltenham Festival in 2003

ANOTHER IRISH FAMILY WITH horseracing in their blood is the Walsh dynasty. Set up by Rupert Walsh, the family's racehorse-training yard in Kill near Dublin provided his son Ted with the encouragement and opportunity to become a top jockey.

He won the Irish amateur title before turning professional, but it was as a trainer that he would enjoy his greatest success. His first winner after retiring from the saddle was Rock De Prince who triumphed in the 1991 Thyestes Chase but it was in the 2000 Martell Grand National that he hit the headlines. Ridden by his son Ruby, who was debuting in the race, joint-favourite Papillon held on in the run-in to win by one and a quarter lengths from Mely Moss. Ted still successfully trains racehorses and is also a familiar face as a television pundit.

Born on 14 May 1979 in County Kildare and named after his grandfather, Rupert 'Ruby' Walsh soon found himself being described as the young pretender to Champion Jockey Tony McCoy's throne.

Having won the Irish amateur title at 18, he turned professional and claimed the Irish championship boasting a grand total of 96 winners. The 1999-2000 season was not kind to him, however, with a broken collarbone and two broken legs keeping him out of the saddle for much of the campaign. These setbacks didn't prevent the father and son partnership from registering a victory in the Irish

Grand National on Comanche Court at Fairyhouse. With this triumph coming just two weeks after their Aintree success on Papillon, the Walsh family certainly had cause to celebrate.

Ruby returned the following season to regain his Irish title. He and Papillon again joined forces in the 2001 Grand National but on a soggy track they could only manage to be the final one of the four finishers. Fourth place beckoned again in the following year's Aintree showpiece, this time on Kingsmark, but he made amends by winning the 2002 Scottish National on Take Control.

Ruby won his second Grand National in 2005 on Hedgehunter and was crowned Champion National Hunt Jockey in Ireland for a third time the same year. Indeed, in the 2004-05 season he almost won all four Nationals, triumphing on Numbersixvalverde in Ireland and Silver Birch in Wales but was just beaten by Joe's Edge by a head in the Scottish on Cornish Rebel. Ruby and Hedgehunter failed in their attempt to be first to retain the title when they could only manage second in the 2006 Aintree Grand National, six lengths behind Niall Madden on Numbersixvalverde.

Weatherbys

THE NAME WEATHERBY, WITH ITS horseracing connections, dates back to the eighteenth century – 1770, to be precise, when Mr James Weatherby took up the post of secretary at the Jockey Club. His industry and business skills were complemented by his nephew whose expertise was in the area of pedigree racehorses. In 1791 James was largely responsible for the publication of the General Stud Book, which took a view on four hundred horses and thereby set the standard for thoroughbreds around the world.

Weatherbys themselves recognise that their core business has been in place since 1800, their administrative skills being essential for the smooth running of horseracing in general.

Apart from the regular updating of the General Stud Book, Weatherbys are answerable to the British Horseracing Board for the registering of colours, horses names and recording handicap details. All runners are to be entered via them, as they issue the final riders and runners for each race. They also collect and distribute the prize money for all British races. Nobody in racing can exist without coming into contact with Weatherbys.

Financial services can also be offered via their own bank, although this is not limited to the racing fraternity.

RIGHT Roger Weatherby, who runs Weatherbys Bank

BELOW A childhood portrait of James Weatherby, who founded the company in 1770

Weight

THE WEIGHT PROBLEM THAT jockeys constantly have to battle with will never go away for, by the very nature of the sport, horses which are built for speed could not possibly perform without a lightweight on top. In 2006, this became a contentious issue when the Irish racing authorities raised the maximum riding weight of a flat jockey to eight stone four pounds from seven stone twelve pounds, but the British Horseracing Board refused to follow suit. This left many unhappy riders who are finding it increasingly difficult to come in under eight stone.

The unnatural existence they lead, often involving sweating in saunas and denying themselves anything but the odd piece of chicken garnished with a lettuce leaf, has never been a healthy one. In modern times the very fact that *homo sapiens* has naturally grown in stature makes it even less of an attraction. Some current flat jockeys are as tall as five feet eight inches.

A number of apprentices have to give up on their dream due to lack of gastronomic discipline or outgrowing their chosen sport. This is less of a problem in National Hunt racing, where the jockeys will weigh in at a couple of stone heavier than their flat-racing counterparts.

ABOVE Jockeys are carefully weighed to ensure they conform to regulations

Walwyn

FULKE WALWYN, ALONG WITH Fred Winter and Algy Anthony, remains one of the few Grand National heroes who have both ridden and trained a winner of the Aintree race.

Having started riding as an amateur jockey in 1929, Walwyn won the 1936 National on Reynoldstown, before he embarked on an amazing training career which saw him complete the other leg of his Aintree double when Team Spirit, ridden by Willie Robinson, won the 1964 race.

For just over 50 years Fulke Walwyn trained the cream of National Hunt racing from his Saxon Lodge Stables in Lambourn. He won his first Cheltenham Gold Cup in 1952 when Dorothy Paget's Mont Tremblant, ridden by Dave Dick, won at 8/1. He won a further three Gold Cups with Mandarin in 1962, Mill House in 1963 and the Dikler in 1973, who won by a short head after a gigantic tussle with Pendil.

In the same year as Mandarin won the Gold Cup, he also went on to win the Grand Steeplechase de Paris, ridden by the great Fred Winter with a broken bit and rudderless for most of the race. Two Scottish Grand Nationals were won, while two Champion Hurdles followed in 1962 and 1965 with Anzio and Kirriemuir.

On the death of Peter Cazalet, Walwyn took over as the Queen Mother's trainer with great success. He trained over 150 winners for her, the victory of Special Cargo in the 1984 Whitbread Gold Cup the highlight.

Walwyn trained over 2,000 winners during his illustrious career, 44 of which were at the Cheltenham Festival. He died in 1992.

X-Codes

THERE IS A FASCINATION FOR horses that excel in both codes of racing, able to transfer their skills from the warm, sunny days of the flat to the mud-splattered, hard-bitten winter game. Sea Pigeon was one such horse. As a three year-old he ran seventh in the 1973 Derby before going north to eventually arrive at Peter Easterby's yard, where hurdling became his game.

A hard-pulling horse, he gradually learned to settle, and to good effect, finishing fourth in the Champion Hurdle before taking the Scottish Champion in 1977. Reverting to the flat, he won the Chester Cup the same year and completed that double a year later. He won the competitive Ebor Handicap (1979) carrying 10 stone on the flat before winning two Champion Hurdles at Cheltenham (1980-81). John Francome claimed he was the best horse he rode.

Brown Jack was another great horse who started his career on the flat by finishing last on his debut in 1927. A fat, lazy horse, he enjoyed himself and started to improve. Sent over hurdles, he finished third on his debut, then won five in a row before winning the Champion Hurdle in 1928.

Reverting to the flat and ridden by the brilliant Steve Donoghue, he became an outstanding stayer, winning the Ascot Stakes at Royal Ascot and then six consecutive Queen Alexandra Stakes. He was enormously popular with the public.

ABOVE Sea Pigeon gets a warm reception from the crowd at Cheltenham in 1981

X-Factor

IN ALL SPORTS, THERE EXISTS A group of competitors who have just that little bit extra to offer, and it's not something you can acquire. It may manifest itself in sheer innate ability, the will to overcome seemingly insurmountable odds or simply through personality or charisma. This is the X-factor, and racing has had its fair share of such horses.

By all accounts Ormonde, the unbeaten English Derby winner at the back end of the nineteenth century, must have had it, as did his famous jockey Fred Archer, and Mill Reef from the early 1970s definitely qualifies as a star performer.

RIGHT Frankie Dettori certainly has star quality

BELOW Mill Reef putting in a great performance to win the 1971 Epsom Derby

In more recent years, the much-loved grey Desert Orchid, who still gets to parade at major meetings, captured the public's imagination with his bold jumping, winning ways and sheer physical presence.

The late lamented Best Mate, winner of three Cheltenham Gold Cups, produced a similar reaction from race-goers, as did the hugely successful Arkle, whose jumping is legendary.

Amongst jockeys, the 'housewives' favourite' Lester Piggott may have not had bags of charisma but, once on a horse, his skills were almost otherworldly. Looking at the current crop, Frankie Dettori with that huge smile and bubbly personality, not to mention his ability, is definitely X-factor material.

Yard

THE WORD YARD IS USED in racing circles to describe the premises used for training purposes. More commonly, the word stables will suffice and these come in varying sizes.

All premises must meet strict guidelines as laid down by the racing authorities and no trainer can function without the necessary permit or licence. Either the trainer or a trusted member of staff has to be either on the premises or close to them at all times.

Owners send their horses to these stables expecting the best possible results from the trainer and his underlings plus a degree of care that anyone would expect for an animal that may be worth hundreds of thousands of pounds.

A large training stable may have over two hundred horses in residence

at any one time, smaller concerns little more than a handful. A trainer is not limited to handling horses for just one owner. Larger set-ups might employ an assistant trainer plus a whole team of stable staff.

Some yards can go long periods without achieving those sought-after wins, others will go through purple patches but the objective is to keep every animal fit at all times. Occasionally this goal can be thwarted by a stable virus or the dreaded 'cough'.

ABOVE A traditional English yard with stables in the background

Zafonic

THE LIFE OF ZAFONIC IS A MIXTURE of tragedy and triumph. After emerging from a successful juvenile season, he won the 2,000 Guineas at Newmarket in 1993 with a devastating burst which blew his rivals away and broke the course record which had stood for 45 years. This singled him out as a very special animal with much more to come.

His relatively short career, in which he only ran seven times, producing five victories, came to an abrupt halt after a disappointing run in the Sussex Stakes where it was reported that he had burst a blood vessel. His brief but significant track appearances had realised prize money of over £500,000.

At stud his success continued, in 1997 he became the leading first season sire, his progeny producing 25 wins, with the star turn being Xaar, the leading European juvenile of the year.

Sadly, Zafonic's destiny was not to prove a happy one, for having been leased out to Arrowfield Stud in New South Wales by Juddmonte Farms in 2002, he died in a freak accident when falling over a gate. His devastated ex-trainer Andre Fabre described him as '…a fantastic horse…a fabulous individual.'

RIGHT Zafonic after winning the 2,000 Guineas at Newmarket in 1993

BELOW Zafonic in action in the same race

The pictures in this book were provided courtesy of the following:

GETTY IMAGES
101 Bayham Street, London NW1 0AG

EMPICS
www.empics.com

Thoroughbred Photography

Book design and artwork by Newleaf Design

Published by Green Umbrella

Series Editors Jules Gammond, Tim Exell, Vanessa Gardner

Written by Jonny Whetstone and Claire Welch with Peter Gamble and Ian Welch

Picture Research by Philip Raby

Also available on DVD

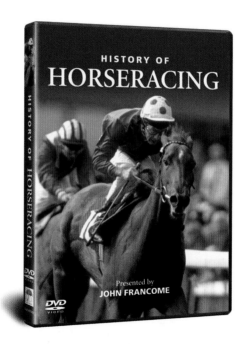

Available from all major stockists of DVDs or online at:
www.greenumbrellashop.co.uk